**Discover how much you
really know
about how the other half—
vampires and witches,
the exotic and erotic—lives!**

- What is the difference between the Dark Gift and the Dark Trick?

- After being revived, Ramses went to the same city in which Marius discovered Those Who Must Be Kept. What city is it?

- What was Louis's name for the death of his victims?

- On what famous New Orleans street corner does Ancient Evelyn see the ghost of Julien Mayfair?

- Roquelaure is one of Anne Rice's pen names. What character in *The Vampire Chronicles* actually wears a roquelaure?

THE
ANNE RICE
TRIVIA
BOOK

Katherine Ramsland

BALLANTINE BOOKS • NEW YORK

Grateful acknowledgment is made to Anne Rice for permission to reprint from the following works of Anne Rice published by:

Alfred A. Knopf, Inc.: *Interview with the Vampire* copyright © 1976 by Anne O'Brien Rice, *The Vampire Lestat* copyright © 1985 by Anne O'Brien Rice, *The Queen of the Damned* copyright © 1988 by Anne O'Brien Rice, *The Tale of the Body Thief* copyright © 1992 by Anne O'Brien Rice, *The Witching Hour* copyright © 1990 by Anne O'Brien Rice, *Lasher* copyright © 1993 by Anne O'Brien Rice, *Taltos* copyright © 1994 by Anne O'Brien Rice, *Cry to Heaven* copyright © 1982 by Anne O'Brien Rice.

Arbor House Publishing Co., Inc: *Exit to Eden* copyright © 1985 by Anne Rampling, *Belinda* copyright © 1986 by Anne Rice writing as Anne Rampling.

Simon & Schuster, Inc.: *The Feast of All Saints* copyright © 1979 by Anne O'Brien Rice.

Ballantine Books: *The Mummy: Or Ramses the Damned* copyright © 1989 by Anne O'Brien Rice.

ISBN 0-345-39251-5

Manufactured in the United States of America

First Edition: December 1994

10 9 8 7 6 5 4 3 2 1

For Anne Rice

Contents

Acknowledgments

Although I had already gathered most of this material by writing other books, Gail Zimmerman offered a very dedicated hand with *Belinda* trivia, and I wish to thank her for her enthusiastic help.

I also want to thank Peter Borland and my agent, Lori Perkins, for getting the ball rolling, and my editor, Joanne Wyckoff, for bravely taking on this project while we were still in the midst of *The Witches' Companion*. I'm also grateful to Andrea Schulz for her availability, assistance, and thoughtful comments, and to Claire Ferraro for her enthusiasm.

Several people who listened patiently as I tested out trivia on them, others who obtained material for me that I needed, and a few who helped with *The Vampire Companion* and *The Witches' Companion* deserve to be noted here. My deep appreciation goes to Sally Broussard, Donna Johnston, Robin Miller, Ruth Osborne, Sue Quiroz, Steven Ramsland, Michelle Spedding, and Linda Westfeldt.

The person who contributed most, both in terms of material and support, quite obviously, is Anne Rice. Her cooperation with each of my books, and her willingness to supply fresh material at a moment's notice, gave this book an added richness. And, after all, she is the one who makes this trivia come alive. Many thanks, Anne.

THE
ANNE RICE
TRIVIA BOOK

INTRODUCTION

Anyone who has read the novels of Anne Rice cannot fail to be impressed by the wealth of details with which she creates her settings and characters. She thoroughly researches and fully renders historical, geographical, and mythological contexts so that her characters can move through fictional worlds rich in nuance and possibility. Because Rice pays careful attention to such things as street names, types of buildings, room decor, and characters' backgrounds and personalities, there is more than enough trivia to be found in her work to fill at least one book. I thought it would be fun to put this material into a quiz format so fans could challenge themselves and each other to discover how much they really know about one of their favorite authors.

This book is divided into two parts. The first part, "The Dark Universe," covers the four novels of *The*

Vampire Chronicles, the three novels of *Lives of the Mayfair Witches*, *The Mummy*, and two vampire-related short stories. I chose not to organize the questions by novel because I wanted to emphasize the coherence of the unified supernatural realm that Rice has created. Although *The Vampire Chronicles* are quite distinct from *Lives of the Mayfair Witches*, many elements of the Dark Universe unite the two. Rice herself explains this best:

The Dark Universe of the witches and the vampires forms one basic fabric because of the belief in spirits—discarnate entities, some evil, some good—who can interfere with mankind. For example, Maharet's description in *The Queen of the Damned* of the spirit world is logically consistent with what Petyr van Abel says in *The Witching Hour* about the nature of the spirits. Beings exist who do not have bodies that we can see, but whose bodies are nevertheless organized and governed by separate rules. These spirits are a form of matter that we just can't measure and understand yet.

There is no magic per se. The Dark Universe is under an umbrella of science consistent with the latest theories of spiritualism, which suggest that entities exist who 'vibrate' at a different rate and have different organizing rules, that they are here with us. The vampires are a pure mutation of spirit and flesh, created by the ability of a spirit to move into the cells and develop parasitically through the blood. And in both realms—that of Lestat and that of Ashlar and Lasher—there are strong hints of other mutations of spirit and flesh on this earth, other mammalian beings who look human but aren't. The Talamasca, of course, links the two universes, knowing of both vampires and spirits, and compiling information on them.

What unites the Dark Universe philosophically is that all of my books are about outsiders. They are about how to be a good human, and they deal with people who feel shut off from their own humanity, who are groping to be more human or who are faced with the terrible choice between power and goodness. The vampires are glittering outsiders, animated by an evil spirit, but they are linked forever to their human souls and consciences. They pay a price for immortality. Witches play with fire when they play with spirits; they want what spirits know, but again and again they pay a hell of a price for it.

Translate this into modern pragmatic terms: How do men and women deal with 'near-death experiences'? How do they deal with a strong instinctual belief that there are guardian angels? How do they achieve sanctity while remaining reasonable? How do they move civilization forward without bowing to superstition and to religions that demand total submission? That is what my Dark Universe is about. There are invisible things there. Metaphorically, they can be seen as tulpas of our imagination. That is, if the world has no ghosts, no angels, no Almighty, then all these beings are the persona of our longing for goodness, for good power, and for command over our bodies and fates. Our moral progress must embrace the world of the spiritual, the unseen, the occult.

Rice's Dark Universe includes (but is not limited to) vampires, witches, spirits, ghosts, mummies, Taltos, the Little People, and the scholars who study them all, the Talamasca. The first chapter, "The Savage Garden," covers the general background and traits of these inhabitants of the Dark Universe. The first section of Chapter One is an overview in which I include a few basic questions about each of the creatures, even though most of the entities have their own sections or chapters later in the book. The second section of Chapter One is about spirits, particularly Lasher, because spirits form the backbone of the Dark Universe. Since Lasher was the spirit of a Taltos, and his organizing force is similar to theirs, the next section focuses on the Taltos, particularly Ashlar. I've also included a section that emphasizes how supernatural powers, such as telepathy and astral projection, join the various entities (including the Talamasca), because these powers are a key feature of the Dark Universe: possessing them offers a means to transcend the human condition but also places those who exercise these powers outside the typical bounds of humanity. And lastly, I deal with the immortal being known as Ramses the Damned, or the mummy; he, too, grapples with issues of supernatural powers versus his humanity.

Rice creates an especially great wealth of detail and characterization for the vampires, witches, and Talamasca, so I have devised separate chapters for each of these beings. Sections within these chapters include questions about central characters.

The next five chapters of Part I quiz readers on the geography, historical events, artistic allusions, and myth and religion of the Dark Universe. These sections really get down to the nitty-gritty! The final chapter asks readers to identify quotes from the novels. Some are obvious, but several quotes require great familiarity with the finer details of the characters' backgrounds and philosophies.

Part II features questions about Anne Rice herself and her nonsupernatural works. She wrote two historical novels, *The Feast of All Saints* and *Cry to Heaven*, right after *Interview with the Vampire*; under the name Anne Rampling, she published *Exit to Eden* and *Belinda*. Although Rice also wrote three pornographic novels as A. N. Roquelaure, they are not included in this book. Rice views them as distinct from her other novels and feels they require separate treatment. Many of the answers to the questions about Anne Rice can be found in my biography of Rice, *Prism of the Night*, and in newspaper and magazine interviews, while others were provided to me by Anne herself. The answers to these questions may not always be apparent, but they are often entertaining.

The careful reader will note that some answers that seem elusive at first will become clear when details from other questions are added. For example, I may ask for the name of a character that the reader does not immediately recall, but that same name may show up in another question. A few answers are deliberately planted for those who are very alert. Although all of the answers are provided at the back of the book, I suggest looking things up in the novels first. It's more fun.

Each chapter ends with some difficult bonus questions, but the real challenge can be found in the Super Bonus Questions in Part III. Readers who can answer even half of these questions can consider themselves experts. They're tough!

So open up to "The Savage Garden" and have fun!

PART I

The Dark Universe

In the Dark Universe that Anne Rice creates exist beings with unusual characteristics and powers. Spirits, ghosts, vampires, witches, mummies, Taltos, and the Little People all experience the world from their own unique perspectives, yet they are joined by a set of rules that govern the imaginative realm in which they live. Concerned with questions of love and hate, good and evil, and life and death, they rely on their own special resources to survive, gain power, and maintain their integrity. Each of the following chapters addresses some type of entity within, or some facet of, Rice's supernatural realm.

CHAPTER ONE

The Savage Garden: Night Creatures and Dark Powers

What Lurks in the Dark Universe: An Overview

Short Answer

1. What does Lestat mean by the term "Savage Garden"?
2. What are the principles, according to Lestat, that govern the Savage Garden?
3. Who coined the term "Children of Darkness"?
4. Who were the Children of the Millennia?
5. What is distinctive about a vampire's finger-nails?
6. What is the difference between the Dark Gift and the Dark Trick?
7. By what phrase did Lestat refer to the vampire's

journey from the trappings of mortality to the experience of immortality?

8. Who first coined the phrase mentioned in question 7?

9. When Louis questioned Armand about the meaning of their existence, he referred to a figure in a picture in Armand's room. Who was that figure?

10. To refer to Armand's seductive power, Lestat used the same term for a female demon that Petyr van Abel used for Charlotte Mayfair's allure. What is it?

11. What did the tribe of the twins do with their loved ones' corpses?

12. Before he joined the Talamasca, David Talbot apprenticed himself to an unusual type of shaman in Brazil. What was the name of her religion?

13. Raglan James claimed there are two kinds of souls. Name the primitive one.

14. What made Ramses' elixir of immortality work most potently?

15. Jesse read the books of Ian Stevenson in her work for the Talamasca. What phenomenon did Stevenson describe?

16. Of what heinous crime did Ashlar accuse the Little People when he met them in Donnelaith, shortly after he heard Yuri's story?

17. What primitive custom involving the Yule Log did Lasher witness?

18. How did Lasher realize that he was definitely not human?

19. What was the term for the genetic abnormality that allowed witches to mate with a Taltos?

20. What was the Devil's Knell?

21. Why would a creature like Lasher, after he had become a Taltos, leave no fossil residue upon death?

22. *Daoine Sith* is another name for the Little People. What does it mean?

23. Who seemed to be the leader of the group of Little People that included Fyne, Rogart, and Robin?

24. Give one of the theories about how the Little People came into existence.

25. Name one of the places in Scotland to which the Edinburgh professor whom Julien consulted compared the frightening tales of Donnelaith.

True or False

___ 1. When Marius described other types of immortals to Lestat, he included Ramses.

___ 2. Lasher could possess Aaron Lightner only when Aaron was asleep.

___ 3. According to folklore, leaving out saucers of milk would appease the Little People and the Taltos.

___ 4. Sluagh is another name for the Taltos.

___ 5. Stuart Gordon thought Tessa was a reincarnation of one of the Little People.

___ 6. The Little People could breed with the Taltos.

___ 7. Stuart Townsend was possessed by the ghost of a woman who had been a prostitute in Paris.

___ 8. David Talbot's name for a pesty spirit was astral tramp.

___ 9. The Little People lured the Taltos with drums.

___ 10. Lasher was mistaken for the Nyades Road ghost.

___ 11. Stuart Townsend was possessed for fifteen years.

___ 12. Father Louvier's book on demons was titled *Malleus Malificarum.*

___ 13. Maharet claimed that the human species' primary enemy is the abstract divorced from the material.

___ 14. Maharet told Jesse that ghosts are quite powerful and should be avoided at all cost.

___ 15. Marius advised Lestat to keep his vampire children as human as possible.

The Spirit World:
Ghosts and Discarnate Entities

Short Answer

1. How do spirits like Amel differ from ghosts?
2. What, according to Mekare, links spirits to the natural order?
3. How does a spirit make a human immortal?
4. How does a spirit become self-conscious?
5. Whose ghost warned Arthur Langtry to leave New Orleans?
6. What did Lasher tell Julien he must do in order to remain earthbound?
7. What kind of ghost did Jesse see that was *not* the ghost of a person?
8. What ghost appeared to Jesse just before she was made a vampire?
9. What is unusual about the DNA of spirits like Amel and Lasher?
10. When did Claudia first appear as a ghost?
11. What did Lestat decide about Claudia's spirit?
12. Whose ghost plagued Louis when Louis was a mortal?
13. Who thought Armand was a ghost?
14. What physical features attract ghosts to humans, according to Maharet?
15. From Maharet's description, how might spirits affect the course of human evolution?

16. With which internal organ did Akasha believe Amel had fused to make her a vampire?
17. Why are spirits unable to permanently possess corpses?
18. What, according to Maharet, is the essential source of the spirits' attraction to humans?
19. What do spirits envy about humans?
20. What did Amel do that disturbed the twins' mother?

Lasher

Short Answer

1. What symbol did Suzanne use to call Lasher forth in the circle of stones?
2. How long had Lasher been hovering in chaos over the circle of stones in Donnelaith?
3. In what guise did Lasher appear to Suzanne?
4. At what time did Lasher first appear to Rowan?
5. How did the Mayfairs and their Garden District neighbors refer to Lasher?
6. What did the Talamasca conclude about Lasher when they reviewed his patterns throughout the Mayfair history?
7. Who was the first person that Lasher possessed in his drive to become flesh?

8. What was Marie Claudette's defense against Lasher's "private" voice?
9. Rice originally intended to have Lasher appear in another book she was writing, but he grew beyond it in her imagination. Which novel was it?
10. Who was Lasher's father in Lasher's fifteenth-century incarnation?
11. Who did Lasher's father think Lasher was?
12. Where did Lasher study to become a priest?
13. In what area of Donnelaith did the Protestants stone Lasher to death?
14. What was the promise Lasher made to the Mayfair witches?
15. When Lasher materialized for Rowan on Christmas Eve, as whom did he initially appear?
16. What was the Talamasca's first indication that Lasher could manipulate people to do his will?
17. Who was the Italian whore who invited Lasher, as a priest, to taste the sins of the flesh?
18. What was odd about Lasher's head when he came into the flesh?
19. What did Michael Curry find on Lasher when he put Lasher into a grave?
20. Where is Lasher's grave?

Multiple Choice

___ 1. Lasher's modes of attack included all of the
following except
A) Pitching corpses
B) Seduction
C) Hallucination
D) Exploiting fears
E) Pricking the skin

___ 2. Lasher took Rowan to all of the following
cities except
A) Berlin
B) London
C) Paris
D) Geneva
E) Rome

___ 3. Lasher's design for becoming flesh involved
all of the following except
A) Mating brother to sister
B) Educating Michael Curry
C) Sending Rowan to San Francisco
D) Possessing Julien
E) Building First Street

___ 4. Lasher appeared in a photo with which witch?
A) Mary Beth
B) Stella
C) Antha
D) Deirdre
E) Julien

___ 5. Lasher used each of the following aliases except
A) Frederick Lamarr
B) Samuel Newton
C) Lester Dunogud
D) Oscar Aldric Tamen

___ 6. Lasher is involved, or is suspected to be involved, in the deaths of which of the following?
A) The Comte de Montcleve
B) Aaron Lightner
C) Tyrone McNamara
D) Cortland Mayfair
E) Peter Mayfair
F) Bertha Marie Becker
G) Sister Bridget Marie
H) Victor Gregoire
I) Petyr van Abel
J) Lord Mayfair
K) Deirdre Mayfair

L) Alicia Mayfair
M) Dr. Samuel Larkin
N) Gifford Mayfair
O) Carlotta Mayfair
P) The Earl of Donnelaith
Q) Richard Llewellyn
R) Sister Daniel
S) Lionel Mayfair
T) Stella Mayfair

Taltos

Fill in the Blank

1. If a Taltos successfully mates with a human, the gestation period before birth is about _____ months.
2. Ashlar's tribe called a being that is part human and part Taltos a _____.
3. When the Taltos settled Donnelaith, they lived in tall structures called _____.
4. Prior to Lasher, a Taltos born into the Mayfair family was called a _____.
5. To pose as a human tribe, the Taltos called themselves _____.
6. The type of writing that the Taltos used was called _____.

7. Stuart Gordon located Tessa in the country of

_____.

8. Stuart Gordon showed Tessa to Marklin and Tommy inside a historical structure known as

_____.

9. The man who helped Emaleth right after she was born was named _____.

10. Emaleth gave Rowan _____ to heal her.

Short Answer

1. What was the origin of the Taltos name?
2. How did the Little People get Lasher to make a new Taltos?
3. How did the Taltos who survived the Holy Battle of Donnelaith reduce their threat to the humans that lived near them?
4. Ashlar mentioned a Taltos form of suicide that began with one of their favorite activities. What was it?
5. Ashlar referred to a mythical figure of great destruction when he described for Rowan what the regeneration of the Taltos race could mean for humankind. Who is this figure?
6. When the Taltos lived in the lost land, what was the fate of any member of the tribe who fatally injured another or who defied the rules?
7. After Janet cursed Ashlar, he saw a vision of her

in a cave. The vision altered the curse somewhat.
How was it changed?

8. How can a Taltos detect a witch?

9. Of what use were the Little People to the Taltos after the Taltos adopted the identity of a human tribe?

10. What myth-related fear of Emaleth's was alleviated after she was born?

11. Why did Stuart Gordon believe King Arthur might have been a Taltos?

12. What was one of the Celtic names for the Taltos?

13. What was the title of the manuscript written by the Talamasca after Ashlar's visit?

14. Stuart Gordon's search for the Taltos had in common an ambition similar to a more ancient activity associated with the Taltos. What did Ashlar call this ancient activity?

15. How is Janet's curse connected with Lasher?

16. What did Ashlar call the manner in which Taltos told and retold their history?

17. What did the Taltos call their manner of reasoning with one another?

18. Ashlar described a piece of jewelry found in Sutherland, Scotland. What does it depict?

19. Where did Stuart Gordon want to bring together a male and female Taltos?

20. Where was the lost land of the Taltos located?

Ashlar

True or False

___ 1. Ashlar was born on the island known as the lost land.

___ 2. Ashlar became the leader of the Taltos tribe in Britain because of his heightened visual perception.

___ 3. Ashlar had a son with Janet.

___ 4. Of the Little People, Ashlar befriended only Samuel and Aiken Drumm.

___ 5. In the genealogy that the Edinburgh professor showed to Julien, there were several Ashlars mentioned, one of whom was married to Queen Mora.

___ 6. In the same genealogy, King Odin was listed as Ashlar's father.

___ 7. Ashlar commissioned Miss Paget to make dolls for his museum that spun around.

___ 8. Although the Taltos decided to place lintels on top of the standing stones of Stonehenge, Ashlar preferred not to have them.

___ 9. Samuel called Ashlar's company Toys Without Limit.

___10. The surname Ashlar uses is Templeton.

___11. Columba converted Ashlar on Iona.

___12. Ashlar gave the Talamasca the history of his people that he wrote for Columba.

21

___13. Ashlar wanted to build parks on top of towers for people to enjoy.

___14. Jacob is Ashlar's night pilot.

___15. Ashlar drank from Chalice Well on his pilgrimage.

___16. To seal their friendship, Ashlar sent Michael Curry a carousel horse.

___17. Ashlar appeared in Mona's dream.

___18. The Cathedral of Donnelaith contained the relics of St. Ashlar's clothing.

___19. Ashlar claimed that the Taltos experienced two levels of reincarnation.

___20. Ashlar wanted a bulldog he could name Samuel.

Short Answer

1. In what city does Ashlar live?
2. Who is Ashlar's female assistant?
3. Who is Ashlar's manservant?
4. When Ashlar decided to check out the problems with the Talamasca, in what London suburb did he establish his office?
5. What is the title of the book that Ashlar wrote?
6. After leaving Claridge's, what was Ashlar's first stop in Donnelaith?
7. What were Ashlar's final instructions to Yuri?
8. Which member of the Talamasca did Ashlar kill?

9. What did Ashlar take with him from the Talamasca Motherhouse in London?

10. Where did Ashlar eat his final meal with Samuel before Samuel returned to Donnelaith?

Supernatural Powers

Multiple Choice

___ 1. Each of the following Mayfairs was part of Mona's healing circle for Rowan except

A) Fielding
B) Paige
C) Randall
D) Lily
E) Clemence

___ 2. Each of the following exhibited telepathic abilities except

A) Rowan Mayfair
B) Mona Mayfair
C) Yuri Stefano
D) Mary Jane Mayfair
E) David Talbot

___ 3. The Mayfair witches credited with the power of bilocation include all except

A) Julien

B) Charlotte

C) Mary Beth

D) Cortland

___ 4. Rowan had a series of precognitive dreams during her initial involvement with Lasher. The following people all appeared in these dreams except

A) Rembrandt

B) Caravaggio

C) Karl Lemle

D) Petyr van Abel

E) Jan van Abel

___ 5. Maitland Mayfair and his son both died soon after which of the Mayfair witches predicted their deaths?

A) Mary Beth

B) Julien

C) Stella

D) Marie Claudette

E) Marguerite

___ 6. Where did Lestat first experience astral projection?

A) Miami
B) New Orleans
C) Georgetown
D) Lynkonos
E) Haiti

___ 7. Lestat first learned the power of flight in

A) Miami
B) New Orleans
C) San Francisco
D) Paris
E) The Auvergne

___ 8. The following are all vampire abilities except

A) Great speed
B) Telekinesis
C) Telepathy
D) Stretching their limbs great distances
E) Healing wounds

___ 9. Lestat thinks the power of flight is terrible for vampires because

A) They get cold
B) They lose their humanity
C) They experience disequilibrium
D) They can't breathe
E) They get airsick

___10. Aaron Lightner's paranormal abilities included

A) Telekinesis
B) Psychometry
C) Bilocation
D) Precognition
E) Shape-shifting

Short Answer

1. How did Landing Smith provoke Mary Beth to use one of her supernatural powers?
2. Stella, Mary Beth, and Antha all used coins from a velvet purse that had a peculiar reputation. What was so unusual about this purse?
3. Michael Curry awakened from his near-death experience with the power of psychometry, the ability to gain visual impressions about an item or a person via touch. How did Alexander, in the Talamasca, use this same power?
4. What was Aaron Lightner's "calling card"?
5. Mitch Flanagan suggested that the presence of the giant helix in members of the Mayfair family may have a specific marker. What was his hypothesis?
6. Aaron Lightner discovered via psychic means that Deirdre Mayfair was not suffering. Describe how he did this.

7. What do the vampires call their ability to block mind readers from probing?
8. What did Louis mean by the term "vampire eyes"?
9. What supernatural ability did the twin witches, Mekare and Maharet, possess before they became vampires?
10. What does the term "spellbind" mean?

The Mummy

Short Answer

1. What did Lawrence Stratford see that made him exclaim, "This is no tomb!" when he entered what he believed to have been the burial tomb of Ramses the Second?
2. In which time period did Lawrence Stratford awaken Ramses?
3. Elliott Savarell's title of nobility dated back to King Henry VIII. What is it?
4. When Alex proposed marriage to Julie and she refused his offer, they were dancing to a Strauss waltz. Name it.
5. Where did Ramses find his "lost love"?
6. Who was Daisy Banker?
7. What was Lawrence's name for the library in his home, where Ramses was displayed?

8. What was Alex's official title while his father was still alive?

9. What famous museum in London did Julie and Ramses visit together?

10. Who was Meneptah?

11. Julie booked passage for herself, her maid, and Ramses through which famous English travel agency?

12. What did Ramses want to visit in Abu Simbel, Egypt?

13. Ramses contrasted what he observed all around him in the modern world with the dominant theme of ancient times. What was this theme?

14. Who was Charlotte Whitney Barrington?

15. Ramses, Julie, and their party remained in Alexandria only a short while, staying at a famous resort frequented by wealthy Europeans. Name it.

16. Where did Ramses lay dormant for three hundred years before Cleopatra woke him to gain his help?

17. What did Zaki, Samir's cousin, do to make money?

18. Samir taught Julie how to disguise herself as a man. After he dressed her, he explained to her what she must do. What were his instructions?

19. Which early Egyptian king called on Ramses to help him?

20. How did Elliott finally acquire the elixir of immortality?

Fill in the Blank

1. The elixir of immortality was hidden among poisons that _____ had once tried as a method of suicide.
2. Ramses' reign as a mortal king of Egypt lasted _____ years.
3. _____ was Henry Stratford's Egyptian mistress.
4. Alex mentioned a poem about Ramses II by _____ that he had learned in school.
5. _____ was the French café in the Arab Quarter in Cairo where Elliott urged Ramses to meet with him concerning Cleopatra and the elixir.
6. _____ was Julie's butler.
7. Cleopatra went out with a young tourist to see _____, one of the Seven Wonders of the Ancient World.
8. Samir discovered a liqueur, _____, in a French café in Cairo, that quickly became his favorite.
9. Of the four cars that Elliott owned, he favored the _____.
10. Julie's house was located in the London district known as _____. (Hint: Rice used this name again in another novel).

Savage Garden Bonus Questions

1. On his trip to Donnelaith, after listening to Yuri, Ashlar approached the Little People in the glen. What did he smell before he spoke to them?

2. What did the Little People claim they do to Talamasca scholars who come into the glen of Donnelaith?

3. To mate with a particular female, Ashlar claimed he once had to beg permission from how many Taltos?

4. What did Deborah Mayfair say about Lasher that surprised Petyr van Abel?

5. Where did Dr. Petrie first see Lasher's name?

6. How did Michael Curry realize that his poolside vision of the Mayfair witches probably originated with Lasher rather than with the "earthbound dead"?

7. What reason did David Talbot give for the Talamasca's origin?

8. What did Mael call ghosts?

9. What did Amel fling at Khayman's house to torment him for raping the witches Mekare and Maharet?

10. What did Mael give to Jesse before she left Maharet's compound?

CHAPTER TWO

Vampires:
The Children of the Night

Multiple Choice

___ 1. What property is *not* attributable to a vampire's unusual blood?

A) It has the power to heal
B) It is combustible
C) It has the power to addict a mortal
D) It can become invisible
E) It can confer immortality

___ 2. The nemeses of the vampires include all but which of the following?

A) Falling in love with a victim
B) Boredom
C) Change
D) Fire
E) Drowning

___ 3. Lestat referred to the vampire realm by all of the following names except

A) Dark Court
B) Erebus
C) Elohim
D) The Evil Undead

___ 4. At the Gathering of the Immortals in Maharet's compound, which of the vampires did Akasha describe as the most predatory?

A) Louis
B) Lestat
C) Maharet
D) Marius
E) Gabrielle

___ 5. Which of the following superstitions about vampires did Louis admit was true?

A) They can turn into steam and go through keyholes
B) They can be killed with stakes driven through the heart
C) They cannot see themselves in mirrors
D) They can be repulsed by religious icons such as a crucifix
E) They must avoid the sun

32

___ 6. Which is an inaccurate paraphrase of the Dark Rules that Armand spelled out for Lestat and Gabrielle?

A) Only the coven leader can work the Dark Trick
B) All who receive the Dark Gift should be beautiful
C) The oldest vampires should make the new vampires
D) No vampire, except the coven leader, must ever destroy another vampire
E) No vampire should reveal his name or his history to a mortal and allow the mortal to live

___ 7. The Legend of the Twins was found in all of the following places except

A) A 6,000-year-old vase in Berlin
B) A desert cave in southern Mongolia
C) Egyptian papyrus
D) A cave in Palestine
E) Clay tablets in England

___ 8. Raglan James, in Lestat's vampire body, killed in all of the following places except

A) New York
B) Bal Harbor, Florida
C) Dominican Republic
D) Curaçao
E) Martinique

___ 9. The Fang Gang taught Baby Jenks about each
of the following except
A) Coven houses
B) Healing fang wounds
C) The astral plane
D) The vampire history
E) The best type of victim

___10. All of the following are Lestat's rock videos
except
A) "Those Who Want to Die"
B) "The Dance of les Innocents"
C) "Those Who Must Be Kept"
D) "The Legacy of Magnus"
E) "Age of Innocence"

Matching

Match the vampires to their preferred style of killing:

A. Lestat
B. Armand
C. Louis
D. Khayman
E. Claudia

___ 1. Killed in a savage frenzy, then broke the bones and sucked out the marrow.
___ 2. Gently seduced victims who desired death.
___ 3. Used pretense to gain advantage over unwitting victims.
___ 4. Prolonged the experience, loving the wallop of the heart as it stopped.
___ 5. Waited until hunger was overwhelming, then killed quickly.

Match the characters to the mortal ages at which they became vampires:

—— 1. 5	A. Eric
—— 2. 14	B. Marius
—— 3. 17	C. Claudia
—— 4. 20	D. Lestat
—— 5. 25	E. Louis
—— 6. 29	F. Baby Jenks
—— 7. 32	G. David Talbot
—— 8. 35	H. Jesse
—— 9. 40	I. Daniel
——10. 74	J. Armand

Short Answer

1. How old was Armand when Louis first met him?
2. After Gabrielle became a vampire, what did she learn about her hair that upset her?
3. What happens to the bloodthirst as a vampire ages?
4. Who told Pandora that she could find Marius in the frozen north of the New World?
5. Rice's short story for *Playboy*, "The Art of the Vampire at Its Peak in the Year 1876," was introduced as having what source?
6. What was the surprise twist of that story?
7. What was another way that the vampires referred to the First Death?

8. Why did Maharet have more difficulty seeing with "vampire eyes" than did other vampires?

9. In Rice's short story "The Master of Rampling Gate," Julie discovered a vampire living at her family's 400-year-old estate. Why did he make the choice to become a vampire?

10. In the same story, how did Julie save the estate from destruction?

11. In what year did "The Master of Rampling Gate" take place?

12. What was the name that Marius used for Armand when he painted him, and what does it mean?

13. Armand gave Daniel an amulet to protect him from other vampires. What did it contain?

14. What did Maharet do to Akasha in Antioch?

15. Armand told Louis the reason killing other vampires was a capital crime. What was it?

16. What did Lestat find in a prison cell in Magnus's tower?

17. Who put Akasha and Enkil into the sun?

18. How long did Louis drink animal blood before he drank from Claudia?

19. Where did Marius finally reunite with Armand?

20. How many vampires were in the First Brood?

21. Who accompanied Pandora to rescue Marius?

22. Where does Gabrielle sleep?

23. Where did Louis hide from the vampires who

wanted to kill him after the reporter published his confession?

24. What was Jesse's most dangerous assignment from the Talamasca?

25. Where did Lestat make David a vampire?

26. Who predicted the coming of a Dark Monarch of destruction among the vampires two centuries before Akasha went on her brutal rampage?

27. What percentage of mortal men did Akasha wish to kill?

28. What kept Marius interested in existing for a thousand years?

29. Which of Lestat's music videos did Khayman favor?

30. Where did the vampires recover after Akasha's death?

Fill in the Blank

1. As vampire bars and "safe" houses sprang up around the world, they were organized under the name of _____.

2. The Fang Gang's slang for vampire was _____ _____.

3. Louis, Claudia, and Lestat lived together for _____ years.

4. Armand considered himself, religiously, to be a _____ of evil.

5. The vampires' "Declaration" against Lestat was written on the walls of _____.

6. The Druid vampire's burnt condition was due to what he called the _____.

7. When Lestat first saw Akasha, he used a _____ to wake her.

8. Before she killed Lestat, Claudia placed white _____ in a vase.

9. Raglan James booked the _____ suite aboard the QE2.

10. The Fang Gang slang for entrancing mortals was _____.

11. Before they realized their first pursuers in Paris were vampires, Lestat and Gabrielle referred to them as _____.

12. The vampire that Akasha chose to be the first martyr to her cause was _____.

13. Lestat told the survivors of Armand's eighteenth-century Parisian coven to become _____.

14. The name of the deceased woman in Eastern Europe who had become a vampire's victim was _____.

15. The vampire who failed to receive the dream of the twins was _____.

16. In Lestat's dream of the tiger, he saw it take a _____ from David.

17. There were as many as _____ vampires in the Theater of the Vampires when Louis and Claudia arrived.

18. _____ claimed to have been a vampire in another life before being born as a mortal.

19. _____ made a videotape of himself in his coffin so he could watch his hair grow.

20. When the mortal Daniel discovered the house he believed was Lestat's, he found a _____ that confirmed it for him.

21. The Fang Gang liked to dance in _____.

22. Armand cut off the hands of _____.

23. Marius discovered Armand as a mortal boy in a _____.

24. Marius was made a vampire during the Druid celebration called _____.

25. _____ pushed Lestat from a tower in Paris when Lestat sought his help with Louis.

26. Twelve-year-old _____ was Baby Jenks's first victim.

27. Khayman recited poetry to mortals who sat on a _____ in his room.
28. Marius kept a pen of _____ outside his arctic wasteland shrine for Akasha and Enkil.
29. Maharet called her mortal descendants the _____
_____.

30. David Talbot's new body had belonged to a _____ -year-old mechanic.

The Dark Realm from Louis's Perspective

Short Answer

1. To how many people had Louis told his story before he told it to the boy reporter?
2. Why did Lestat make Louis a vampire, according to Louis?
3. What did Louis have to do to prove he was serious about becoming a vampire?
4. After Louis's experience sharing a coffin with Lestat, where did he find a place to sleep alone?
5. After Louis became a vampire, he used what kind of illness as an excuse for avoiding the daytime functions of his mortal relatives?
6. What neurosis did Louis suffer that was magnified, particularly in Paris, when he was a vampire?

41

7. How did Lestat demonstrate that Louis could live off animal blood?

8. Why did Lestat warn Louis not to drink from victims after the heart stopped?

9. From what kind of human victims did Louis refuse to take blood?

10. Who was Louis's mortal love?

11. What became of Louis's mortal love as a result of her contact with him?

12. Louis and Claudia discovered that peasants in Eastern Europe used an animal to locate the grave of a vampire. What kind of animal was it?

13. What did Claudia and Louis call the vampires they saw in Eastern Europe?

14. Which vampire was made first, Louis or Santiago?

15. In what section of Paris did Louis first encounter Santiago?

16. Armand told Louis several ways a vampire could die. Which was false?

17. What did Claudia tell Louis Armand wanted from her?

18. What did Armand do that nearly destroyed Louis's passion?

19. What did Louis use to cut off Santiago's head?

20. Where did Louis and Armand go together in Paris after Louis destroyed the Theater of the Vampires?

21. Where did Louis reunite with Lestat in 1985?

22. Who accompanied Louis to Maharet's compound?

23. What did Jesse reveal that sent Louis back to New Orleans?

24. By what religious term did Louis refer to his vampire existence?

25. What did Louis say to Akasha?

The Dark Realm from Lestat's Perspective

Short Answer

1. Why did Lestat make Louis a vampire, according to Lestat?

2. How did Lestat discover that Louis had told their story to a reporter?

3. What was the name of the rock group that Lestat joined?

4. What did Claudia use to poison Lestat before she stabbed him?

5. How many times has Lestat been shot by a gun in *The Vampire Chronicles*?

6. Who is Lestat's American lawyer?

7. When Lestat first introduced himself to mortals that he needed as agents, he created a false identity. From where did he claim to come?

8. Who was Lestat's first mortal agent?

9. Who was Lestat's first vampire "child"?

10. What kind of dogs did Lestat have as a mortal?

11. When Lestat became mortal again after being a vampire, he made love to a nun named Gretchen. What was the significance of her name?

12. What was the name of Lestat's German shepherd?

13. Lestat rode the same brand of motorcycle as Baby Jenks. What was it?

14. According to Louis, Lestat befriended a musician in New Orleans. Who was this musician's benefactor?

15. What time of day did Lestat hate as a mortal?

16. What is Lestat's favorite type of material to wear?

17. What physical benefit did Lestat gain from going into the sun in the desert?

18. How many wolves did Lestat kill?

19. What popular singer's music influenced the way Rice wanted Lestat's voice to sound? (Hint: It is *not* the one that Baby Jenks names.)

20. Where did Lestat hold his rock concert?

Multiple Choice

___ 1. Shortly after Gabrielle became a vampire, she said to Lestat, "Disaster, my son." She was referring to
A) Armand's coven
B) The death of her husband
C) Making Nicolas into a vampire
D) Armand's plea to join them
E) Her hair

___ 2. Which of the following does Lestat *not* refer to as a "vampire's city"?
A) Miami
B) Venice
C) Paris
D) Amsterdam

___ 3. Who was Lestat's lover on the Parisian stage when he played Lelio?
A) Flaminia
B) Eleni
C) Celeste
D) Luchina
E) Isabella

___ 4. When Lestat and Nicolas engaged in a drunken discussion, Lestat named the moment of supreme clarity

A) The Golden Moment
B) The Dark Moment
C) The Age of Reason
D) It
E) The Witching Hour

___ 5. When Akasha went on her rampage, whose dreams did the vampires receive?

A) Maharet's
B) Akasha's
C) Lestat's
D) Enkil's
E) Mekare's

___ 6. What decision did Lestat make at the age of twelve?

A) To become a vampire
B) To become an actor
C) To go into a monastery
D) To kill wolves
E) To get a pair of dogs and start a kennel

___ 7. Lestat drives a
A) Red Porsche
B) Black Porsche
C) Black BMW
D) Silver Bentley
E) Black Jaguar X16

___ 8. Lestat's favorite flower is
A) Rose
B) Lily
C) Queen's Wreath
D) Bougainvillea
E) Wisteria

___ 9. Which of these is *not* one of Lestat's favorite
     hotels?
A) Ritz in Paris
B) Claridge's in London
C) Hassler in Rome
D) Royal Court in New Orleans
E) Stanhope in New York

___10. How much money did Lestat lose to Raglan
     James's clever computer skills?
A) $10,000
B) $25,000
C) $1 million
D) $10 million
E) $20 million

Vampire Bonus Questions

1. In *Interview with the Vampire*, Lestat's killing near a haunted house inspired tales of what supernatural entity?

2. In Louis's dream aboard ship, what did his sister place on his grave?

3. What word did Armand give Louis as an amulet against the other vampires in Paris?

4. The development of Magnus was influenced by what short story?

5. Who was the imaginary fiancée that Lestat invented to cloak his thoughts from Raglan James?

6. What did Louis do with Armand's coffin when they parted in New Orleans?

7. What was the metaphor that Maharet used to explain how vampires are attuned to one another?

8. What did Santino give to Jesse that disappeared within days?

9. What was Azim's name for Marius?

10. What did Lestat first give Gabrielle from Magnus's hoard?

CHAPTER THREE

Witches: The Mayfair File

Facts from the Mayfair History

Matching
Match the Mayfair with his or her identifying trait or situation:

___ 1. Antha

A. Offered to adopt Deirdre after Antha died

___ 2. Gerald

B. Ryan's mistress

___ 3. Young Pierce

C. Caught bouquet at Rowan's wedding

___ 4. Mary Beth

D. Lived on Esplanade Avenue in New Orleans

49

___ 5. Stella   E. Frequently sat with Rowan while she was in a coma

___ 6. Corrington   F. Her ghost told Michael she was not "one of them"

___ 7. Barbara Ann   G. Julien's New York business contact

___ 8. Mona   H. A "Mayfair's Mayfair"

___ 9. Mary Jane   I. Acquired the Mayfair emerald

___10. Deborah   J. "La Petite Gypsy"

___11. Augustin   K. Interested in family history of insanity

___12. Charlotte   L. Died from a fall down the First Street stairs

___13. Marguerite   M. Was told to burn down the First Street house

___14. Cortland   N. Gave birth to a Taltos before Rowan did

___15. Magdalene   O. Died by Julien's hand

___16. Clytee   P. Died of a uterine hemorrhage

___17. Ida Bell   Q. Held prisoner at Amelia Street

__18. Granny	R. Wanted to establish a sugar refinery
__19. Ancient Evelyn	S. Twenty-fold Mayfair
__20. Beatrice	T. Died by swallowing his tongue
__21. Hamilton	U. Mistakenly believed to be dead for several years
__22. Katherine	V. Legacy designee who lost the status
__23. Kelly	W. A lawyer who supported Mayfair Medical
__24. Lionel	X. Filled the pool with champagne
__25. Claire Marie	Y. Sold a poem to *The New Yorker*
__26. Clemence	Z. Evelyn's mother
__27. Cornell	AA. Often cross-dressed as a man
__28. Clancy	BB. Mary Beth inscribed "Fear No More" on his grave
__29. Belle	CC. Initiated construction of the First Street house
__30. Eileen	DD. Witnessed Beatrice's marriage to Aaron

Fill in the Blank

1. The Mayfair emerald originated in the country of _____.

2. Deirdre asked her friend, _____, to call Aaron Lightner to help her.

3. _____ Mayfair administered the Julien Mayfair Trust Fund for Donnelaith.

4. The Mayfair law firm moved from Camp Street to _____ Street in the business district of New Orleans.

5. Stella gave Evelyn _____ to wear, which ended up in Stella's secret hiding place.

6. Cortland's accomplice used _____ to try to poison Aaron Lightner.

7. Mary Jane travels to and from Fontevrault on a boat called a _____.

8. The last witch doll was made from the bone and hair of _____.

9. The female witch doll dressed in trousers depicts _____.

10. Deirdre was drugged with strong doses of _____ _____.

Short Answer

1. Julien claimed to be Antha's father. Why is this impossible?

2. How did Carlotta try to get rid of the Mayfair emerald?

3. What did Cortland tell Michael Curry in Michael's vision of the Mayfair witches?

4. How old was Deborah when Suzanne was burned as a witch?

5. What was the clan of Donnelaith's original name, according to a source that Julien read in Edinburgh?

6. For whom did Carlotta work?

7. How many generations of Mayfairs actually lived on the Maye Faire plantation in Saint-Domingue?

8. How many jars did Marguerite fill with body parts during her experiments with Lasher?

9. Which Mayfair witch had no storm when she died?

10. What effect did Charlotte's birth have on Deborah's trial as a witch?

11. What happened to Sister Daniel after she expelled Deirdre from St. Rose de Lima's for being seen in the nuns' garden with a man?

12. Katherine's behavior involved Julien in a duel. What did she do?

13. How did Nancy come to live at First Street?

14. What was the Riverbend plantation's actual name?

15. What was Mary Jane's method of self-education?

16. How much property was designated for Mayfair Medical?

17. Who painted the portrait, acquired by the Talamasca, of Antha wearing the Mayfair emerald?

18. Although the Talamasca claimed that Peter Mayfair, Jeanne Louise's twin, never spelled his name in the French manner, it did show up in some records as Pierre. Where?

19. How did Stella interpret the concept of "the thirteen"?

20. Why was Petyr van Abel allowed to take Deborah out of Donnelaith?

21. What function did the witchpricker serve at Deborah's trial for witchcraft?

22. Where did Lasher seduce and kill Gifford Mayfair?

23. Who was the priest who heard Deirdre's confession that she had seen the Devil?

24. What strange event happened regularly at the Mayfair crypt?

25. Who was the architect of the First Street house?

Multiple Choice

___ 1. Each of the following was (or was suspected
to be) Julien's lover except
A) Mary Beth
B) Richard Llewellyn
C) Belle
D) Sister Bridget Marie
E) Daniel McIntyre
F) Christian

___ 2. Samples of genetic material involving Rowan
and Lasher were sent to all of the following
institutions except
A) Keplinger Institute
B) DNA, Inc.
C) International Genome
D) Genetic Institute of Paris

___ 3. After doing genetic research, Dr. Larkin com-
pared the Mayfair family with each of the fol-
lowing except
A) The Amish
B) The Mormons
C) The Wilkes family in *Gone with the Wind*
D) The Mafia
E) The Carringtons on "Dynasty"

___ 4. Which witch officially established the legacy?
A) Marie Claudette
B) Mary Beth
C) Angélique
D) Jeanne Louise
E) Deborah

___ 5. The legacy wealth included all of the following except
A) Shopping malls in Boca Raton
B) Oil leases
C) The Mayfair emerald
D) The First Street house
E) The Mona One mutual fund

___ 6. The law firm that became Mayfair and Mayfair was
A) Byrnes, Brown, and Blake
B) McIntyre, Murphy, Murphy and Mayfair
C) Fleming and Mayfair
D) Carondelet, Inc.
E) McIntyre, Byrnes and Mayfair

___ 7. Angélique married
A) Tyrone McNamara
B) Henri Marie Landry
C) Daniel McIntyre
D) Vincent St. Christophe
E) Arlington Kerr

___ 8. When Antha ran away to New York, she
supported herself by selling

A) Stella's pearls

B) Mary Beth's velvet purse

C) The Mayfair emerald

D) Ancient gold coins

E) An antique locket with a miniature of a dark-
haired child

___ 9. Which witch appeared to Lasher when Michael chased him up to the third-floor bedroom at First Street?

A) Suzanne

B) Deirdre

C) Antha

D) Stella

E) Deborah

___10. Each of the following is cited as a witch's
mark except

A) A sixth finger

B) A giant's height

C) Hair inside the ear

D) A birthmark like a mole

E) Red hair

Julien Mayfair

True or False

___ 1. Stuart Townsend's body was stored in Julien's former bedroom.

___ 2. Julien knew seven languages by the age of fifteen.

___ 3. To remain earthbound, Julien put his hair and fingernails underneath his mattress.

___ 4. One of Julien's former lovers ran an antiquarian bookstore.

___ 5. Julien's belief that Lasher was not the Devil came from reading Rousseau.

___ 6. Julien tried to run over Michael Curry with a car to get him to return to New Orleans.

___ 7. In Michael Curry's vision, Julien appeared as one of the Mayfairs who was part of the pact with Lasher.

___ 8. Julien always had his picture taken in front of the keyhole doorway at First Street.

___ 9. After Julien died, he appeared to Evelyn at Amelia Street.

___10. Julien had the ability to project a younger image of himself into another place.

1. How did Julien realize his grandmother's ghost was not a real ghost?

2. In Mona's dream, Julien told her to change her hair ribbon to what color?

3. What did Evelyn tell Julien that inspired him to remain earthbound?

4. What was the name of Julien's daughter with Suzette?

5. How did Julien characterize his sons in relation to himself?

6. What did Julien believe Lasher to be?

7. What did Julien want to purchase from the Edinburgh professor?

8. What relation to Julien was Michael O'Brien?

9. Before Storyville opened where did Julien go with Katherine to have fun in New Orleans?

10. What did Lasher tell Julien the day Mary Beth was born?

Michael Curry

Short Answer

1. What is Michael's full name?
2. How old was he when he first met Rowan?
3. As a boy, Michael saw Lasher away from First Street on which two occasions?
4. In what part of New Orleans did Michael grow up?
5. What did Michael's father do?
6. What famous violinist did Michael see in concert?
7. What was the first opera that Michael saw when he went to San Francisco?
8. What great childhood fear did Michael conquer after nearly drowning in the pool at First Street?
9. Where did Michael go to college?
10. What were the names of Michael's two San Francisco girlfriends before he met Rowan?
11. Who took care of Michael after his near-death experience in San Francisco?
12. Who found Michael's St. Michael medal by the pool at First Street?
13. What does Michael love to collect?
14. What is the name of Michael's construction company?
15. Why did Julien have difficulty getting Michael's attention?

16. What was Michael's physical vulnerability?
17. Where did Michael read the Talamasca file on the Mayfairs?
18. After his near-death experience, why did Michael want to meet Rowan?
19. How is Michael related to the Mayfairs?
20. What did Michael use to kill Lasher?

Multiple Choice

___ 1. Michael was swept into the ocean near a restaurant called
A) Bojangles
B) Cliff House
C) Santa Fe
D) Ocean View
E) Grady's Oyster Bar

___ 2. Michael recalled that all of the following were in his near-death vision except
A) A doorway
B) A jewel
C) A dark-haired woman
D) A number
E) A crypt

___ 3. All of the following are titles of Michael's books except
A) *History of the Frame House in America*
B) *San Francisco's Grand Ladies*
C) *Victorian Architecture*
D) *Grand Victorian Inside and Out*

___ 4. Mona compared Michael to
A) Lord Byron
B) Charles Dickens
C) Pip
D) David Copperfield
E) Darius, King of Persia

___ 5. Michael's favorite composer is
A) Beethoven
B) Bach
C) Verdi
D) Vivaldi
E) Bartok

Rowan Mayfair

True or False

___ 1. Rowan worked at University Hospital.

___ 2. Rowan's boat was called *The Wind Singer*.

___ 3. Rowan first met her relatives at a funeral home called Lonigan and Sons.

___ 4. Father Lafferty baptized Rowan.

___ 5. The first person Rowan killed telekinetically was a girl named Mary Jane.

___ 6. Aaron Lightner first spoke to Rowan in front of Michael Curry's house.

___ 7. Rowan was educated at San Francisco State University.

___ 8. Karl Lemle's fetal experiments inspired Rowan to go into medical research.

___ 9. Rowan was born November 7, 1959.

___10. Rowan escaped from Lasher by knocking him out with a porcelain vase.

___11. Rowan's vision for the legacy included building Mayfair Medical.

___12. Lasher first appeared to Rowan in Destin.

___13. The Talamasca's file on the Mayfairs horrified Rowan.

___14. Ashlar saved Rowan's life by killing Stuart Gordon.

___15. After she heard Ashlar's story, Rowan wished she had spared Emaleth's life.

Mona Mayfair

Fill in the Blank

1. _____ Mayfair informed Mona that she was the legacy designee.
2. Mona's mother was _____ Mayfair.
3. Rowan first saw Mona at _____.
4. Mona fell in love with _____ from the Talamasca.
5. Mona wanted to baptize her baby at _____.
6. Mona seduced her cousin David in front of the _____
7. Mona gave birth to her baby at _____.
8. Rowan thought Mona should marry _____ Mayfair.
9. Mona was _____ years old when she had her baby.
10. Mona went to school at _____.
11. Gifford referred to Mona by the biblical name _____
12. Ancient Evelyn wanted to give to Mona _____ _____
13. Granny Mayfair told Mona that Mona once had a _____ that was removed.
14. At Rowan's wedding, Mona was the _____ _____
15. _____ told Mona she was pregnant.

Witches Bonus Questions

1. How many Grady Mayfairs are mentioned in the Talamasca file?
2. Why did Carlotta want to tear out Antha's eyes?
3. What was suspicious about Nancy Mayfair's death?
4. In Michael Curry's vision of the Mayfair witches, who sat beside Marie Claudette's bed?
5. Of Deborah's sons, which was the firstborn?
6. What was Julien's greatest fear about remaining earthbound?
7. To what historical figure did Richard Llewellyn compare Julien when they went together to Lulu's Mahogany Hall in Storyville?
8. What piece of music, aside from Julien's record, did Michael want to play for Rowan when she was in a coma? (Hint: It figures in another novel as well.)
9. Julien was reputed to have killed his tutor near Riverbend for gossiping about the Mayfair family. From what city did this tutor come?
10. In what kind of car did Julien ride to rescue Evelyn from Amelia Street?

CHAPTER FOUR

The Experts: The Talamasca

Short Answer

1. The Talamasca founder had something in common with the vampire Magnus. What was it?
2. What was the founding principle of the Talamasca?
3. Who first claimed that the purpose of the Talamasca was to rescue the Taltos and bring it back as a species?
4. Who was the first Talamasca member that Lestat encountered?
5. Which member brought Jesse into the Order?
6. Who wrote the first document of the Mayfair file?
7. How was Petyr van Abel disguised when he rode into Donnelaith?
8. What occupation would Petyr van Abel have

pursued had he not become a member of the Talamasca?

9. How did Erich Stolov describe Clement Norgen's and his function in the Mayfair case?

10. How did Aaron Lightner nearly acquire the Mayfair emerald?

11. Who shot Yuri Stefano?

12. What did Marklin George call Stuart Gordon's plan to mate two Taltos?

13. What did the Order do with Marklin and Tommy after Stuart died?

14. Who sold Rembrandt's painting of Deborah Mayfair to the Talamasca?

15. What vampire painting is in the Talamasca archives in London?

16. Which vampire gave a warning to David Talbot and Aaron Lightner at Lestat's rock concert?

17. What language did the Talamasca often use to record their activities in code?

18. What did "the Dutchman" offer to Lasher to try to lure him to Amsterdam?

19. Who replaced Anton Marcus as head of the Order?

20. What rule did David Talbot break that caused concern in the Order?

21. What Mayfair event did Arthur Langtry witness?

22. What made Carlotta get a restraining order against the Talamasca?

23. How did the Talamasca receive a written message from Stella?
24. Where did Rice first see the word "Talamasca"?
25. The Talamasca was wrong about which of the following facts?

__A. The father of Antha
__B. Julien's age when he killed Augustin
__C. The records of Lestat's properties in New Orleans
__D. The father of Deirdre's baby
__E. The existence of the man that Julien called Lord Mayfair
__F. Where Cortland died
__G. The ownership of the Theater of the Vampires

Matching

Match the informants and investigators to the information they provided for the Talamasca files:

__ 1. Nathan Brand

__ 2. Amanda Grady Mayfair

__ 3. Beatrice Mayfair

__ 4. Emilie Blanchard

__ 5. Irwin Dandrich

__ 6. Juliette Milton

__ 7. Jan van Clausen

__ 8. Mr. Bordreaux

__ 9. Allan Carver

__10. Dr. Larry Petrie

__11. Owen Gander

__12. Rita Mae Lonigan

A. Investigated Rowan's telekinetic murders

B. Located Antha in New York

C. Described Petyr van Abel's demise

D. Described the storm at Antha's death

E. Provided gossip about Stella's parties

F. Believed Carlotta was dangerous

G. Told Aaron about Deirdre's adolescence

H. Described Cortland's bizarre behavior

I. Collected Mayfair gossip from Beatrice

J. Described Lasher's protection of Deirdre

K. Provided photos of the Mayfairs

L. Described Mary Beth's precognition

69

Match each of the following Talamasca members with the item most closely associated with that person:

___ 1. Joan Cross   A. Enzo's twin

___ 2. Rodolpho   B. Stopped clocks for Deborah

___ 3. Tim Hollingshed   C. Befriended Lestat

___ 4. Martin Geller   D. Assessed Deborah's powers

___ 5. Roemer Franz   E. Saved accused witches

___ 6. Alexander Cunningham   F. Joan Cross's pupil

___ 7. Crawford   G. Visited Donnelaith with the professor from Edinburgh

___ 8. Stefan Franck   H. Decided the fates of Marklin and Tommy

___ 9. Jake   I. Had several titles of nobility

___10. Anton Marcus   J. Succeeded Martin Geller as head of the Order

___11. Evan Neville   K. After Petyr van Abel's death decided that direct contact with Mayfairs was dangerous

___12. David Talbot   L. Corresponded with Petyr van Abel

___13. Richard Kramer   M. Took a bribe and became part of the corruption

___14. Geertruid van Stolk   N. Provided guns and passports for David and Lestat

___15. Junius Paulus Keppelmeister   O. Selected Aaron Lightner to work on the Mayfair file

Multiple Choice

___ 1. The characteristics of demons, according to Petyr van Abel, included all of the following except

A) Aging and dying

B) Growing stronger

C) Possessing bodies

D) High intelligence

E) Lapsing into chaos when their worshipers are gone

___ 2. The Talamasca members associated with Amsterdam included all of the following except

A) Aaron Lightner   D) Alexander

B) Yuri Stefano   E) David Talbot

C) Stuart Gordon

___ 3. The exchange for the Elders' secret fax
number is in
A) Venice
B) New York
C) London
D) Rome
E) Amsterdam

___ 4. All of the following were part of the Grand
Design except
A) Mitchell Flanagan was run over
B) Lasher's tissue specimens were confiscated
C) Aaron Lightner was hit by a car
D) Samuel left Donnelaith
E) Tessa was kept in a tower

___ 5. All of the following events warned Aaron
about problems in the Talamasca except
A) Gifford's clothing was stolen
B) The lab samples from Lasher were stolen
C) Erich Stolov had been with the Talamasca for
only three years
D) The Elders forbade Yuri from joining Aaron
E) The Elders took Aaron off the case

___ 6. The largest Talamasca Motherhouse is in
A) Rome
B) London
C) Amsterdam
D) New Orleans
E) Geneva

___ 7. The Talamasca member with whom Stuart
Townsend fell in love was
A) Elaine Barrett
B) Helen Kreiss
C) Elvera Fleming
D) Joan Cross
E) Nancy Mitford

___ 8. The hotels in which Aaron Lightner stayed
include all of the following except
A) Royal Court
B) Campton Place
C) George and Pilgrims Hotel
D) St. Francis
E) Pontchartrain

___ 9. Stuart Gordon's research included all of the following except

A) Arthurian legends
B) "Lives of the Scottish Saints: Giants"
C) *History of the Taltos of Britain*
D) Folklore about giants
E) "Of Stone Circles and Souterrains"

___10. The name of the Talamasca retreat house outside New Orleans is

A) Oak Alley
B) Oak Haven
C) *Bontemps*
D) *Sans Souci*
E) Font du Lac

Talamasca Bonus Questions

1. Where was the Amsterdam Motherhouse situated?
2. Where was Arthur Langtry buried?
3. What object of value to Lestat was found in the Talamasca archives?
4. To which Motherhouse did Jesse go when she finished her London apprenticeship?
5. How old was Marklin George?
6. Which Motherhouse did Ashlar visit when he grew lonely on his wanderings?
7. Who was Yuri's Talamasca friend in Amsterdam?
8. What was David Talbot's favorite drink?
9. Which Motherhouse did Julien see?
10. A schoolgirl named Liz Conklin described an event associated with Deirdre Mayfair that ended up in the Talamasca files. What did she witness?

CHAPTER FIVE

Religion and Mythology

Gods and Goddesses

Short Answer

1. What god did Ramses share with Enkil?
2. When Enkil and Akasha became vampires, they adopted the identity of what two Egyptian deities?
3. When Lestat performed his rock concert, with which Greek deity did he identify? (Hint: He is the god of the theater.)
4. To which Greek god did Petyr van Abel allude when he discussed with Charlotte the possibility that immortals can die?
5. Whom did David Talbot see arguing in a Parisian café?
6. Akasha called herself a goddess and planned to

restructure the human world, with women as the dominant force. Baby Jenks's religious association upon seeing Akasha foreshadowed Akasha's new role. To whom did Baby Jenks allude?

7. Azim acted as a god in a temple, demanding human sacrifice. Where was the temple located?

8. How did Armand describe God to Louis when Louis believed himself to be a child of Satan?

9. The tribe to which Mekare and Maharet belonged worshiped what form of deity?

10. Marius described a sense of a godlike presence that he wanted to believe in. What did he call it?

11. Who was the fertility goddess that Akasha worshiped before she became Enkil's queen?

12. What did the Good God of the Taltos look like?

13. Who first introduced Ashlar to the Christian God?

14. Why did Ashlar believe that the Christian God was worth his conversion?

15. What Norse god did Mona think of when she saw Michael Curry doing carpentry?

Mythology

Multiple Choice

___ 1. When Mona saw Michael Curry asleep, she referred to him by the name of a figure from a Greek myth. What was the name of the figure? (Hint: Lestat used the same myth to describe Louis as the lover of this sleeping figure.)

A) Actaeon
B) Hercules
C) Endymion
D) Melpomene
E) Apollo

___ 2. Armand and Rowan were both described in terms of a Greek youth whom Zeus favored. What is his name?

A) Ganymede
B) Hyacinth
C) Perseus
D) Sisyphus
E) Theseus

___ 3. Stuart Gordon honored one of the Glaston-
   bury legends whenever he entered or left the
   town. His ritual was to
A) Take a cutting from the Holy Thorn
B) Kiss the crypt of Joseph of Arimathea
C) Stand inside a Druid circle
D) Wash his hands in Chalice Well
E) Walk one mile along the Great Ley

___ 4. Who referred to vampirism as a "white fire
   from the moon"?
A) Akasha
B) Claudia
C) Maharet
D) Gabrielle
E) Mekare

___ 5. When Lestat fled Armand's coven under les
   Innocents, as well as when he fled Raglan
   James after gaining back his body, he cau-
   tioned himself with the imagery from a Greek
   myth not to look back. To what figure did he
   refer?
A) Proteus
B) Theseus
C) Orestes
D) Orpheus
E) Ganymede

___ 6. Lestat viewed Magnus as the figure from a Greek myth who stole fire from the gods. Who was it?

A) Prometheus
B) Hercules
C) Comus
D) Hermes
E) Sisyphus

___ 7. When Michael Curry saw Mona, Mary Jane, and Morrigan standing together, he referred to them as

A) The Holy Trinity
B) The Three Graces
C) The Three Fates
D) The Weird Sisters
E) The Nereids

___ 8. Because of the circumstances of Deborah's birth, she was called

A) A succubus   D) Dis Pater
B) An imp   E) A siren
C) A merry-begot

___ 9. The god associated with the Wild Taltos was
A) Dionysus   D) Osiris
B) Apollo   E) Morpheus
C) Jack-of-the-Green

___10. When Lestat feared that he might not succeed
      in flying, he compared himself to
A) Daedalus   D) Icarus
B) Horus   E) Apollo
C) Hyperion

___11. Daniel referred to a mythological creature
      when describing how Armand pursued him
      around the world. The creature was a
A) Harpy   D) Bat
B) Griffin   E) Ganfer
C) Basilisk

___12. All of the following are names that the Druids
      used for the vampire they kept imprisoned in
      an oak tree, except
A) Good God   D) Lover of the Mother
B) God of the Grove E) Drinker of the Blood
C) The White One

___13. The Celts hunted the Taltos to make them perform their birth ritual. The Celts' favorite time for this activity was during the season that came to be known as

A) Lent
B) Pentecost
C) Christmas
D) Ash Wednesday
E) Feast of all Saints

___14. Lestat likes to read Jeffrey Burton Russell, an authority on

A) Beltane rituals
B) Angels
C) Body switching
D) The Devil
E) Genesis

___15. To which god did Daniel compare Armand's innocent appearance?

A) Cupid
B) Apollo
C) Thor
D) Hermes
E) Dionysus

Religious Images

Fill in the Blank

1. The Catholic sacrament that serves as a metaphor of what happens to mortals when they are transformed into vampires is called _____.

2. The religious day that Claudia mentioned when she brought in the flowers that foreshadowed her plan to kill Lestat was _____.

3. David Talbot cited _____ as the book that contains the secrets of the universe.

4. Gretchen's religious name was _____

5. _____ was described as a "thief in the night," from 1 Thessalonians 5:2.

6. _____ was described as being like Thomas, who had to touch the wounds of Christ to believe.

7. Lasher began his rampage against the Mayfair women on _____.

8. The Cathedral of Donnelaith was originally Cistercian before it was taken over by the order of the _____

9. Joseph of Arimathea brought Christ's _____ to Glastonbury, where Stuart Gordon met his accomplices.

10. The biblical phrase that Lasher used to describe his emergence into the flesh was _____.

11. When Louis tried to deceive Lestat's father, he

alluded to himself as _____ from the Old Testament.

12. David Talbot discussed the biblical book of _____ when he described the Devil's dissatisfaction with his assignments.

13. To affirm for Lestat how special he was, Lestat's father referred to him as _____, the lost son in the Old Testament who was reunited with his father.

14. The biblical metaphor Lestat used to describe his revulsion toward Raglan James is the visit that _____ made to the Witch of Endor.

15. When Louis's hallucination of Lestat's funeral transformed into his brother's funeral, he referred to himself as _____ from the Bible, slayer of his own brother.

Matching

Many saints are mentioned in Rice's novels. Match the saint to the appropriate description:

___ 1. Dominic

A. One of Gretchen's favorites

___ 2. Joan of Arc

B. Saint of the impossible

___ 3. Columba

C. Drank the bathwater of lepers

___ 4. Paul

D. Paul saw him in a vision

___ 5. Michael

E. Converted Ashlar

___ 6. Catherine of Siena

F. Lasher revered and imitated him

___ 7. Francis

G. Mona saw her as a champion of young people; she was executed for heresy

___ 8. Jude

H. An archangel

___ 9. Rose de Lima

I. Petyr van Abel compared himself in his despair

___10. John of the Cross

J. Michael compared his own zeal upon making the decision to find Rowan

Religion and Mythology Bonus Questions

1. As Gabrielle and Lestat traveled around Europe, she mentioned two Greek gods who were dismembered. Name one of them, along with his specific fate.

2. When Jesse was made a vampire, she saw the image of which bloodthirsty god?

3. Khayman thought of himself as a wanderer. He used a name for himself from Egyptian lore that referred to a double or an immortal soul. What is it?

4. What image from Jewish mythology did Daniel apply to Khayman, and Stuart Gordon to Ashlar?

5. What was the religious day on which Deborah Mayfair was scheduled to be burned at the stake?

6. Who is Lestat's favorite expert on comparative religions?

7. The old Comtesse of Montcleve believed that Deborah's witch doll was used in what pagan fertility rituals?

8. Petyr van Abel mentions a religious group in France that was persecuted during the Inquisition. Who were they?

9. What two dieties did the witch judge accuse Deborah of worshipping?

10. From which god did Julius Caesar suggest the Keltoi came?

CHAPTER SIX

The Arts of Darkness

Paintings

Matching
Match the painting to the relevant person or place
(some answers will be used more than once):

___ 1. Rembrandt's *The Anatomy Lecture of Dr. Tulp*
___ 2. Breughel's *Fall of the Angels*
___ 3. Breughel's *Triumph of Death*
___ 4. Rembrandt's *Members of the Draper's Guild*
___ 5. Bosch's *Death and the Miser*
___ 6. Dürer's *Four Horsemen of the Apocalypse*
___ 7. Dürer's *Salvator Mundi*
___ 8. Dionysian Rites, Villa of the Mysteries
___ 9. Goya's *Los Caprichos*
___10. Traini's *The Triumph of Death*

A. Rowan's dream

B. Lasher

C. The subterranean room in the Theater of the Vampires

D. The coven house in the Faubourg St. Germain in Paris, first draft of *Interview with the Vampire*

E. The Rijksmuseum in Amsterdam

F. Armand and Daniel in Pompeii

Film

Match the movie with the appropriate theme (some answers may be used more than once):

___ 1. *All of Me*

___ 2. *Eraserhead*

___ 3. *Great Expectations*

___ 4. *Lust for Life*

___ 5. *David Copperfield*

___ 6. *On the Waterfront*

___ 7. *The Dead*

___ 8. *Time Bandits*

___ 9. *Ironweed*

___10. *Apocalypse Now*

___11. *It's a Wonderful Life*

___12. *Rebecca*

___13. *Dracula's Daughter*

___14. *Suspicion*

___15. *Body and Soul*

___16. *It Lives*

___17. *Fanny and Alexander*

___18. *Blade Runner*

___19. *Vice Versa*

___20. *Company of Wolves*

___21. *Alien*

___22. *Gaslight*

___23. *Death in Venice*

___24. *Kwaidan*

A. The merging of life and death
B. "Fetal films" and social guilt over pervasive abortion
C. Armand's favorite film
D. Body switching
E. Louis's entertainment
F. Michael Curry's inspiration to better his life
G. Lasher's appearance
H. Michael Curry's frame of mind after his near-death experience
I. Lestat ponders the nature of evil
J. Lestat takes several aliases from it
K. Michael Curry admires the architecture
L. Vampire bar named after it
M. Lestat kills an old woman watching it
N. Armand sees an actor who reminds him of Lestat

89

O. Eric brings it to Maharet's compound

P. Selling one's soul

Poetry

Match the poem with the novel in which it is used (some answers may be used more than once, and some not at all):

___ 1. "The Dolls"

A. *Interview with the Vampire*

___ 2. "Texas Suite"

B. *The Vampire Lestat*

___ 3. "Sailing to Byzantium"

C. *The Queen of the Damned*

___ 4. "Garden of Love"

D. *The Tale of the Body Thief*

___ 5. "Rime of the Ancient Mariner"

E. *The Witching Hour*

___ 6. "Elegy"

F. *Lasher*

___ 7. "Ode to a Nightingale"

G. *Taltos*

___ 8. "The Tyger"

H. *The Mummy*

___ 9. "The Devil's Law Case"

___10. Mother Goose rhymes

90

General

Multiple Choice

___ 1. Lestat learned English from all of the following except
   A) *Black Mask*
   B) Shakespeare
   C) H. Rider Haggard
   D) Mark Twain
   E) Ian Fleming

___ 2. The philosopher whose works Louis saw Claudia reading (whom Elvera Fleming also read) is
   A) Plato
   B) Socrates
   C) Kierkegaard
   D) Sartre
   E) Boethius

___ 3. Julien Mayfair claimed to have read all of the following during his youthful education except
   A) *Robinson Crusoe*
   B) *Tom Jones*
   C) Plato
   D) A. N. Roquelaure
   E) Aristotle

___ 4. Carmilla, one of the vampire bars, was named for a short story by

A) Bram Stoker   D) Oscar Wilde
B) Sheridan le Fanu   E) Dr. Polidori
C) Lord Ruthven

___ 5. Stan Rice's poem "Cannibal" opens the third section of *The Queen of the Damned*. Its theme is

A) Fascism
B) Self-destruction
C) Candomble rites
D) The domination of substance by spirit

___ 6. Lestat described Armand in terms of the work of the artist

A) Michelangelo   D) Bosch
B) Raphael   E) Dürer
C) Caravaggio

___ 7. In *The Tale of the Body Thief*, as Lestat pondered opening lines, he mentioned or quoted from each of the following sources except

A) *A Tale of Two Cities*
B) The Bible
C) *Lolita*
D) *The Postman Always Rings Twice*
E) "The Thing on the Doorstep"

___ 8. Each of the following names in *The Tale of the Body Thief* comes from the film *It's a Wonderful Life* except

A) Bailey's
B) Clarence Oddbody
C) Jake's
D) Lionel Potter
E) Martini's

___ 9. When Lestat killed a man who had done him a service, he said, "Goodnight, sweet prince." This quote is from

A) *Macbeth*
B) *Hamlet*
C) *King Lear*
D) *The Tempest*
E) *Othello*

___10. The first story Raglan James gave to Lestat was by

A) M. R. James
B) Bram Stoker
C) H. P. Lovecraft
D) Charles Dickens
E) James M. Cain

___11. Each of the following actors and actresses is named as having some resemblance to one of the Mayfairs except
A) Rutger Hauer
B) Ava Gardner
C) Clara Bow
D) Spencer Tracy
E) Joan Crawford

___12. Each of the following plays of Shakespeare is mentioned, alluded to, or quoted from except
A) *Othello*
B) *The Taming of the Shrew*
C) *Macbeth*
D) *The Tempest*
E) *Hamlet*

___13. At the worst moments of his life, Michael Curry reads
A) *David Copperfield*
B) *A Christmas Carol*
C) *Great Expectations*
D) *Wuthering Heights*
E) *Cry to Heaven*

___14. The book that both David Talbot and Lestat purchased from the same store in Amsterdam was
A) *Faust*
B) *A Tale of Two Cities*
C) *Great Expectations*
D) *The Trial*
E) *The Tale of the Body Thief*

___15. When Lestat approached Nicolas to make him
a vampire, he alluded to the fairy tale of

A) Sleeping Beauty

B) The Ugly Duckling

C) Snow White

D) Cinderella

E) Jack and the Beanstalk

Short Answer

1. When Lestat visited Louis in his Uptown house
in New Orleans, Louis was reading the biography of a famous writer that Julien Mayfair, Michael Curry, and Anne Rice all claim as a
personal favorite. Who is it?

2. Raglan James gave several short stories to Lestat
to introduce him to the idea of body switching. One was "The Eyes of the Mummy." Who
wrote it?

3. Gretchen and Lestat discussed the difficult questions that result from pondering God's nature
and relationship to humankind. What famous author did she cite who has grappled with the same
themes?

4. When Louis saw the furniture that Madeleine
made for Claudia, he described himself as a
character in a novel. Who?

5. Lestat liked to use the phrase "Tomorrow and to-

morrow and tomorrow." Which of Shakespeare's plays is it from?

6. When Ryan Mayfair refused to use Lasher's name, even after the evidence of Lasher became obvious, to what writer did Mona Mayfair compare Ryan?

7. When Lestat tempted David Talbot into becoming a vampire, Lestat saw himself as a literary figure. Which one?

8. Lestat described Gretchen in terms of a specific artist's work. Who is the artist?

9. What southern writer's work influenced Rice's description of Pointe du Lac?

10. Roquelaure is one of Rice's pen names. It is a French word for cloak. What character in *The Vampire Chronicles* actually wore a roquelaure?

Matching
Characters from films and other literary works are often used to describe Rice's characters. Make the appropriate match (some names may be used more than once):

___ 1. Iago
___ 2. Molly Bloom
___ 3. Steerforth
___ 4. Mrs. Danvers
___ 5. Prospero
___ 6. Ariel
___ 7. James Bond
___ 8. Witch of Endor
___ 9. Sorcerer's apprentis
___10. Jezebel
___11. Alice in Wonderland
___12. Pied Piper
___13. Ophelia
___14. Rumpelstiltskin
___15. Father Christmas
___16. Richard Corey
___17. King Lear
___18. Banquo's ghost
___19. Rapunzel
___20. Dr. Frankenstein

A. Petyr van Abel
B. Mona Mayfair
C. Rowan Mayfair
D. Lasher
E. Michael Curry
F. Carlotta Mayfair
G. Lestat
H. Samuel
I. Yuri Stefano
J. Deirdre Mayfair
K. Mary Jane Mayfair
L. Gabrielle
M. Akasha
N. Louis
O. Ancient Evelyn

—21. "The Invisible Man"
—22. Pip
—23. "Father of lies"
—24. Sleeping Beauty
—25. Maxim de Winter
—26. The straw man
—27. Madwoman of Chaillot
—28. Frog Prince
—29. Rip van Winkle
—30. Frankenstein's monster

Arts of Darkness Bonus Questions

1. When Lestat tracked a serial killer who was following an old woman, the woman picked up a novel in a drugstore which Lestat fondly remembered reading. What is the title?

2. Julien taught poetry to the children of a whore at Lulu's in Storyville. Who was the poet?

3. As Mary Beth lay dying of cancer, whose novels did Carlotta read to her?

4. Which of Stan Rice's poems introduces *The Queen of the Damned*?

5. The Talamasca owns portraits of Petyr van Abel painted by two different famous Dutch artists. Name one of them.

6. Which of Jean Cocteau's films does Louis enjoy?

7. What provocative play by Albert Camus did Michael Curry see as a child?

8. After Rowan left him, what poet did Michael Curry quote to describe his state of mind?

9. Lestat described Tough Cookie and himself as what two figures from the Italian commedia dell'arte?

10. To what character from French pantomime did Khayman compare himself?

CHAPTER SEVEN

What Happened When: History and the Dark Universe

Historical Events

Short Answer

1. Name the English queen who gave birth to Lasher.

2. The professor of folklore and history whom Julien located in Edinburgh pointed out that Donnelaith and a once-pagan saint are mentioned in the accounts of what famous eighth-century monk?

3. What early British tribe did Ashlar's tribe most fear?

4. What historical event coincided with Stella Mayfair's death?

5. After Michael Curry heard Julien's story, he had

a dream about which group of people who later figured prominently in *Taltos*?

6. Who was on the English throne when Ashlar was called back to Donnelaith from Italy?

7. After Akasha died, Marius compared Lestat and his penchant for breaking the rules to what famous military leader?

8. Which pope did Ashlar visit on his pilgrimage?

9. When Nicolas suspected that Lestat possessed supernatural powers, he alluded to a famous trial in France regarding witches. What was it?

10. When Lestat was a mortal, what famous person did he see in Paris?

11. What famous composer gave Nicolas violin lessons?

12. What was happening in Europe when Santino was Born to Darkness?

13. What event triggered the Mayfairs' arrival in Louisiana?

14. Whose sermons instigated the Protestant attack on Donnelaith?

15. Petyr van Abel described Charlotte Mayfair as what famous long-haired Englishwoman?

16. The events surrounding which historical religious organization made Aaron Lightner uncomfortable?

17. When did Columba arrive in Iona to convert the Picts?

18. Whose throne could Lasher, as Saint Ashlar, reputedly restore?
19. During what period of history was Marius born as a vampire?
20. What did Armand say about a vampire's relationship to history?

Matching
Match the date to the event:

___ 1. c. 4000 B.C.   A. Ashlar returned to Donnelaith and saw the cathedral

___ 2. c. 3000 B.C.   B. Cortland Mayfair died

___ 3. c. 1000 B.C.   C. Mona Mayfair born

___ 4. 586   D. Julien Mayfair died; Ramses unearthed

___ 5. 758   E. Lasher killed in Donnelaith

___ 6. 1228   F. Mayfair Legacy officially established

___ 7. 1559   G. Aaron Lightner took over Mayfair files

___ 8. 1665   H. First vampires made by Amel

___ 9. 1689   I. Mary Beth died of cancer

___10. 1780   J. Julien and Mary Beth visited Donnelaith

___11. 1789   K. Mississippi River destroyed Riverbend

___12. 1791   L. Ashlar converted to Christianity

___13. 1828   M. Julien Mayfair born

___14. 1858   N. Maharet made Eric a vampire

___15. 1862   O. Lestat made Louis a vampire

___16. 1872   P. Lestat went underground; Stella Mayfair murdered

___17. 1888   Q. First Street built

___18. 1896   R. Claudia attempted to kill Lestat

___19. 1914   S. Magnus made Lestat a vampire

___20. 1925   T. Michael Curry born

___21. 1929   U. Lestat surfaced and read Louis's confession

___22. 1941   V. Lestat's rock concert in San Francisco

___23. 1954   W. Louis told his story to boy reporter

___24. 1959   X. Suzanne Mayfair burned at the stake

___25. 1975	Y. Lasher destroyed clan of Donnelaith
___26. 1977	Z. Talamasca founded
___27. 1984	AA. Akasha and Enkil went into a trance
___28. 1985	BB. Lestat tried to end his existence in the Gobi
___29. 1989	CC. Michael moved back to New Orleans
___30. 1991	DD. Mary Beth born

Historical Bonus Questions

1. Ashlar mentioned a Roman historian who recorded the activities of Agricola, the first Roman commander to enter Scotland. Who was the historian?

2. Deborah Mayfair read the writings of what seventeenth-century Dutch feminist?

3. Ashlar saw a book in a New York store window that contained the form of religious art that he had learned at Iona. What book was it?

4. When did Aaron Lightner become a member of the Talamasca?

5. Who wrote the account from which Marius first learned about the Druids?

CHAPTER EIGHT

What Happened Where: Geography of the Dark Universe

Short Answer

1. The vampire bar Dracula's Daughter was on a famous street corner in what part of San Francisco?

2. What was Lestat's name for the Crescent City Connection, the twin bridges that cross the Mississippi River from New Orleans?

3. After being revived by Lawrence Stratford, Ramses went to the same city in which Marius discovered Those Who Must Be Kept. What city is it?

4. In which European city is the oldest Talamasca Motherhouse located?

5. Enkil and Akasha were the king and queen of Kemet. What does the name Kemet mean?

6. Although Marius found him in Venice, Armand

was originally from another country. From where was Armand kidnapped when he was a boy?

7. Armand's Night Island was modeled on another famous villa. Name it and its location.
8. Where is Night Island located?
9. On separate occasions, both Louis and Lestat took refuge in a cemetery on the outskirts of Paris. Which one?
10. Lestat grew up near the Massif Central in France; name the region where his father's castle stood.
11. In what Egyptian city were the twin witches captured with Khayman after they fled Akasha?
12. During their attempt to retrieve Lestat's vampire body, Lestat and David boarded the *QE2*. From what island did they set sail?
13. In which European city did Lestat and Gabrielle participate in a vampire sabbat?
14. Where did Lestat acquire a German shepherd as a companion?
15. Renaud's House of Thespians, which became the Theater of the Vampires, was located on a Paris boulevard once famous for its many theaters. Name it.
16. What was the first country in Eastern Europe that Louis and Claudia explored?
17. In which desert did Lestat fly into the sun?
18. Ramses wanted to visit Cairo. Of what significance was Cairo to Lestat?

19. The twins Mekare and Maharet grew up in the valley of Mount Carmel, where one set of the "Legend of the Twins" cave drawings was found. On what mountain was the other set found?

20. David Talbot's country house is in what region of England?

21. At which university in Holland was Jan van Abel a surgeon?

22. When Charlotte fled France, it was rumored that she returned to the island from which her husband came. Name it.

23. Where in California was Maharet's secret house in the woods, where she gathered the immortals to stand against Akasha?

24. Of all the places Akasha took Lestat to help her perform her bloody deeds, which was fictional?

25. Name the street in San Francisco where Louis first told his story to the boy reporter.

26. Gabrielle came from where in Italy? (Hint: It is a setting in one of Rice's novels.)

27. Where did Claudia and Louis dump Lestat's remains when they thought he was dead?

28. Where did the Taltos build their most substantial religious monument?

29. Under what famous tree did Rowan give birth to Emaleth?

30. In what mountain range is Montcleve located?

Matching

Match the event with the restaurant associated with it:

___ 1. Café du Monde

A. Michael Curry ate his first elegant meal as a boy

___ 2. Café Centaur

B. Stella dined with Stuart Townsend before he disappeared

___ 3. Caribbean Room

C. Aaron met Rita Mae Dwyer Lonigan to discuss Deirdre Mayfair

___ 4. Galatoire's

D. Rowan ate with the Mayfairs after her mother's funeral

___ 5. Commander's Palace

E. Lestat pondered his last trip to Paris, which ended in tragedy

___ 6. Café de la Paix

F. Lestat listened to Raglan James's proposal to switch bodies

___ 7. Bailey's

G. Jake met Lestat and David Talbot to prepare them for boarding the QE2

___ 8. Desire Oyster Bar

H. Lestat ate his first meal as a mortal after switching bodies with James

___ 9. Martini's

I. James, in the body of David Talbot, met Lestat

___10. Court of Two Sisters

K. Aaron Lightner met with Julien's former lover, Richard Llewellyn

Match the hotel with the event associated with it:

___ 1. Claridge's, London

A. Stuart Townsend checked in

___ 2. Hassler, Rome

B. Cortland tried to poison Aaron Lightner

___ 3. Ritz, Paris

C. Yuri took Andrew to die, then met Aaron

___ 4. St. Francis, San Francisco

D. Lestat tracked a serial killer

___ 5. Royal Court, New Orleans

E. Aaron's New Orleans headquarters

___ 6. George V, Paris

F. David showed Lestat his new body

___ 7. St. Charles, New Orleans

G. Lestat received a videotape from Raglan James

____ 8. Pontchartrain, New Orleans

H. Stolov and Norgen took rooms here

____ 9. George and Pilgrims, Glastonbury

I. Lestat contracted pneumonia

____ 10. Windsor Court, New Orleans

J. Marklin George had an intimate talk with Stuart Gordon

____ 11. Four Seasons, Georgetown

K. Ramses and Julie took rooms

____ 12. Parker Meridien, New York

L. Michael set the mattress on fire

____ 13. Park Central, Miami

M. Rowan and Lasher took rooms

____ 14. Grand Bay Hotel, Miami

N. Yuri met Ashlar

____ 15. Shepheard's, Cairo

O. Dr. Petrie told Aaron a ghost story

Match the vampire bar to the city in which it is located:

____ 1. Carmilla   A. London
____ 2. Dr. Polidori   B. Paris and Athens
____ 3. Lord Ruthven   C. New York
____ 4. Lamia   D. Los Angeles
____ 5. Bela Lugosi

New Orleans

Multiple Choice

___ 1. Louis's gravestone stands in
   A) St. Louis Cemetery
   B) Lafayette Cemetery
   C) Girod Cemetery
   D) Metairie Cemetery
   E) St. Joseph's Cemetery

___ 2. On what famous street corner did Ancient
   Evelyn see the ghost of Julien as she made
   her way to Mona to deliver news of Gifford's
   death?
   A) St. Charles and Amelia
   B) Prytania and Washington
   C) Camp and First
   D) Canal and Bourbon
   E) First and Prytania

___ 3. Claudia first revealed her plan to kill Lestat
   when she and Louis were near
   A) The Bayou St. Jean
   B) Tulane University
   C) Jackson Square
   D) The Happy Hour Theater
   E) Lulu's Mahogany Hall

___ 4. Mary Beth, dressed as a man, first met Daniel
    McIntyre at
A) The quadroon balls
B) Gallatin Street
C) Storyville
D) The Pontchartrain
E) The St. Louis Hotel

___ 5. Louis, Lestat, and Claudia lived in the French
    Quarter, in a town house modeled on
A) The Hermann-Grima house
B) The Gallier House
C) Madame John's Legacy
D) Pitot House
E) The Beauregard-Keyes House

___ 6. While Lestat restored the town house, he
    lived in a penthouse apartment located
    where? (Hint: Julien bought a town house for
    Katherine here, before she insisted on the
    First Street property.)
A) Dumaine and Decatur
B) Bourbon and St. Louis
C) St. Ann and Royal
D) Dauphine and Esplanade
E) Canal and Bourbon

___ 7. The "Spanish hotel" where Lestat and Louis
    took rooms after they fled the burning Pointe

du Lac is the same hotel in which the Mayfairs rented a lavish suite to serve as their
New Orleans base. It is

A) Windsor Court
B) The Monteleone
C) The St. Louis Hotel
D) The Royal Sonesta
E) The St. Charles Hotel

___ 8. The house under which Lestat hibernated in
the twentieth century is on

A) St. Charles
B) Amelia Street
C) Sixth Street
D) Prytania Street
E) Rue Royal

___ 9. Michael Curry grew up in the Irish Channel
on the riverside of Magazine Street. When he
returned to New Orleans after being gone for
years, he wandered into one of the churches
there and pondered his youth. The church is

A) St. Alphonsus
B) Notre Dame
C) Our Mother of Perpetual Help
D) St. Louis Cathedral
E) St. Mary's Assumption

___10. Louis killed a priest in the same church in which Beatrice Mayfair married Aaron Lightner. It is

A) St. Alphonsus
B) Notre Dame
C) St. Louis Cathedral
D) St. Mary's Assumption
E) St. Stephen's

Paris

True or False

___ 1. Rowan and Lasher arrived in Paris from Berlin and stayed in the Ritz, near the Place Vendôme.

___ 2. Lestat's aspiration was to act at the Comédie-Française.

___ 3. In the first draft of *Interview with the Vampire*, Armand's coven had a house in the Faubourg St.-Germain.

___ 4. Louis allowed his portrait to be painted, then killed the artist in the Latin Quarter.

___ 5. Armand's coven chased Lestat and Gabrielle into the famous Sacre Coeur.

___ 6. Lestat's arrival in Paris as a "vampire for a new age" prefigured such changes as the closing of the cemetery of les Innocents.

___ 7. Lestat used his newfound wealth to move Nicolas to the Ile St.-Louis.

___ 8. Lestat encountered Armand at a royal ball in the Tuileries.

___ 9. Renaud's House of Thespians was located on the Champs-Élysees.

___10. Lestat witnessed executions in the Place de Grève.

Matching
Match countries and cities to events:

___ 1. Venice   A. Jesse rejoined Maharet

___ 2. Rio de Janiero   B. Marklin, Tommy, and Stuart met

___ 3. French Guiana   C. Marius was abducted by a Druid

___ 4. Rangoon   D. Akasha destroyed Baby Jenks

___ 5. Glastonbury   E. Louis and Claudia left their ship

___ 6. Montcleve   F. Marius had an art studio

___ 7. Marseille   G. Gretchen was at a mission

___ 8. St. Louis, Missouri   H. Akasha slaughtered mortal males

__ 9. Sri Lanka	I.	David wanted to visit with Louis and Lestat
__10. Vienna	J.	Mekare recorded her history
__11. Chicago	K.	Rowan opened bank accounts
__12. Peru	L.	Rowan grew up
__13. Zurich	M.	Lasher held Rowan prisoner
__14. Tiburon, California	N.	Armand rescued Daniel
__15. Houston	O.	Claudia decided to go to Paris
__16. Varna	P.	Petyr van Abel killed Father Louvier

Geography Bonus Questions

1. What town did Julien and Mary Beth ride through that served as a gateway into Donnelaith?
2. Which of the twin witches was placed in a coffin on the western shore of Egypt?
3. The fictional Hôtel Saint-Gabriel, where Louis and Claudia took rooms when they first arrived in Paris, is based on which actual hotel?
4. What is the secret place Lestat discovered in South America after leaving Gretchen, which he wanted to show to David?
5. To what town did Louis escape after burning down the Theater of the Vampires?
6. In what part of London did Tommy Monohan have an apartment?
7. What Louisiana town is near Fontevrault?
8. What is Samuel's suite number or location in Claridge's?
9. Deirdre Mayfair ran away to an orphanage later purchased by Anne Rice. What is its name?
10. In what part of Edinburgh did Julien and Mary Beth stay?

CHAPTER NINE

Naming Names:
Who's Who?

Matching
Match the aliases to the appropriate description:

___ 1. de Valois

___ 2. Lestan Gregor

___ 3. Jason Hamilton

___ 4. Clarence Oddbody

___ 5. Dr. Alexander Stoker

___ 6. Sebastian Melmoth

___ 7. Eric Sampson

___ 8. Lionel Potter

___ 9. Stanford Wilde

___10. Baron Van Kindergarten

A. Lestat used it as a stage name in Paris
B. Lestat checked into the Ritz with this name

C. Lestat used this name to transfer a large sum of money to Raglan James

D. Lestat used this name for legal purposes, deriving it from a famous author and an architect

E. David Talbot used this name to reserve a cabin for Lestat on the *QE2*

F. Lestat gave Raglan James a passport bearing this name

G. David Talbot's alias for boarding the *QE2*

H. The alias Raglan James used to book passage on the *QE2*

I. Lestat used this name, based on Oscar Wilde's alias, to book a room in London

J. Lestat used this name to make business transactions in Paris, combining the name of an actor with the name of the villain the actor played

Short Answer

1. Name the only Black member of the Fang Gang.
2. Who named the Theater of the Vampires?
3. What was Alicia Mayfair's nickname?
4. What did Louis call Santiago when he first encountered him?
5. How did Suzanne come up with Lasher's name?
6. When Louis first saw Armand in a black cape and tie, he gave him a name. Lestat referred to himself by the same name to Armand's coven. What is it?
7. What does the name mean that Lestat gave his German shepherd?
8. What was Lestat's name for Claudia, chosen for the way she killed?
9. What do vampires call the place they sleep?
10. In order to preserve the vampire commandments, Eleni used code names for vampires when she wrote letters to Lestat. Whom did she call Our Oldest Friend?
11. What did Armand call Lestat when he was trying to goad Lestat to come out from under his house in New Orleans?
12. What did Magnus call Lestat?
13. Armand called the mindless creatures of Eastern Europe "revenants." What does this name mean?
14. At Maharet's compound, who called the vampires there the Secret Order of the Undead?

15. Why do the Mayfair women always keep their surname, even when they marry?

True or False

___ 1. The word *Talamasca* means "animal mask."

___ 2. Armand's name for his favorite type of victim was Those Who Cannot Resist.

___ 3. Mona learned Morrigan's name in a dream.

___ 4. The vampire bar Lord Ruthven was named after the first fictional vampire.

___ 5. Maharet changed her name several times to hide her identity from members of her mortal family.

___ 6. There are three women named Evelyn mentioned in the Mayfair stories.

___ 7. Michael and Rowan named their unborn child after Rowan's previous unborn child.

___ 8. Eleni called Nicolas Our Violinist in her letters to Lestat.

___ 9. The idiot savant who came to New Orleans and inspired Mary Beth's theory about Lasher's intellect was named Blind Tom.

___10. Antha named Deirdre after a tree that was thought to have the power to ward off evil spirits.

Match the name of the mentor with that of the student:

__ 1. Marius
__ 2. Louis
__ 3. Elaine Barrett
__ 4. Stuart Gordon
__ 5. Aaron Lightner
__ 6. Louis Daly
__ 7. Brazilian priestess
__ 8. Mael
__ 9. Mitchell Flanagan
__10. Junius Paulus Keppelmeister

A. Claudia
B. Stuart Townsend
C. Petyr van Abel
D. Aaron Lightner
E. Yuri Stefano
F. Marklin George
G. Marius
H. Lestat
I. David Talbot
J. Rowan Mayfair

Who's Who Bonus Questions

1. What name did Mary Beth use when she dressed as a man and went to Storyville?
2. By what name did the Talamasca know Khayman?
3. What did the Egyptians call vampires?
4. On what continent is the town from which Rice derived Akasha's name?
5. What was Louis's name for the death of his victims?

CHAPTER TEN

Who Said What?

Matching
Match the characters from the list below with their statements (some names may be used more than once):

___ 1. "Let the flesh instruct the mind."
___ 2. "The Dark Trick never brings love, you see, it brings only the silence."
___ 3. "What does it mean to die when you can live until the end of the world?"
___ 4. "I love to break the rules the way mortals like to smash their crystal glasses after a toast."
___ 5. "Get thee behind me, Satan!"
___ 6. "Sheer will had shaped my experience more than any other human characteristic."
___ 7. "I have never had a true purpose. We have no place."

125

___ 8. "What can the damned really say to the damned?"

___ 9. "If you can read the minds of men, you can have anything that you want."

___10. "The Mayfair witches win over those who would hurt them. They always have."

___11. "For ours is the power and the glory, because we are capable of visions and ideas which are ultimately stronger and more enduring than we are."

___12. "Whether we talk of legitimacy, of a soul, of citizenship, or brotherhood, or sisterhood, it is all the same; we long to be seen as true individuals, as inherently valuable inside as any other."

___13. "I am the earthbound dead."

___14. "Don't be a pawn in somebody's game. . . . Find the attitude which gives you the maximum strength and the maximum dignity, no matter what else is going on."

___15. "The future is a fabric of interlacing possibilities, some of which gradually become probabilities, and a few of which become inevitabilities, but there are surprises sewn into the warp and the woof, which can tear it apart."

___16. "Killing is no ordinary act. . . . It is the experience of another's life for certain, and often the experience of the loss of that life through the blood, slowly."

—17. "And what I shall make is Eden ... and it shall be better than nature."

—18. "As long as Mona has her bow ... everything is going to be all right."

—19. "I have thick blond hair, not quite shoulder length, and rather curly."

—20. "I began my erotic adventures when I was eight."

—21. "And when I make it rich, I'm draining and raising Fontevrault. ... You're looking at a future member of the Fortune Five Hundred."

—22. "Concentration is the key to all I do. I draw together."

—23. "What would we be without the capacity to feel physical pain. And this creature, Lasher, has never bled from the smallest wound. ... He is an immoral intelligence ... and that is what I call unnatural."

—24. "If the cells can be grafted and replicate themselves in other human bodies, the entire future of the human race can be changed. We are talking about an end to death."

—25. "I like my little-girl dresses ... they're my disguise."

A. Louis
B. Lestat

C. Ashlar

D. Rowan Mayfair

E. Michael Curry

F. Babette Freniere

G. Claudia

H. Lasher

I. Stuart Gordon

J. Armand

K. The Talamasca

L. Marius

M. Stella Mayfair

N. Carlotta Mayfair

O. Julien Mayfair

P. Akasha

Q. Mary Jane Mayfair

R. Ancient Evelyn

S. Gabrielle

T. Mona Mayfair

U. Nicolas de Lenfent

V. Yuri Stefano

W. Raglan James

X. Emaleth

Y. Morrigan Mayfair

Z. Aaron Lightner

AA. Magnus

BB. Samuel

CC. Pandora

DD. Ramses

From the list of characters above, indicate whom the quote describes:

___ 1. "... no small part of his beauty was his expression. He appeared wonderfully clever and wonderfully curious ... other worldly, yet perfectly normal. Grander than human; but human nonetheless."

___ 2. "What one of us could have such a face? What did we know of patience, of seeming goodness, of compassion? ... A man in the prime of his life at the moment of the immortal gift. And the square face ... its long full mouth, stamped with terrifying gentleness and peace."

___ 3. "And there the coffin lay in our bedroom, where she watched it often by the hour when it was new, as if the thing were moving or alive or unfolded some mystery to her little by little, as things do which change. But she did not sleep in it."

___ 4. "Different from the start, that's what he'd been."

___ 5. "Mary Beth with vinegar in her veins."

___ 6. "We watch. And we are always here."

___ 7. "The vampire was utterly white and smooth, as if he were sculpted from bleached bone, and his face was as seemingly inanimate as a statue, except for two brilliant green eyes that

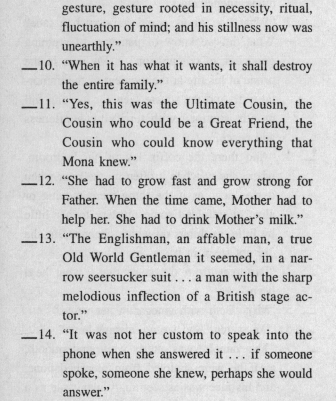

looked down at the boy intently like flames in a skull."

___ 8. "In her earliest pictures she is the image of the luscious child in the Pears Soap advertisements, a white-skinned little temptress."

___ 9. "He had moved to his feet with a body totally at his command, devoid of the habit of human gesture, gesture rooted in necessity, ritual, fluctuation of mind; and his stillness now was unearthly."

___10. "When it has what it wants, it shall destroy the entire family."

___11. "Yes, this was the Ultimate Cousin, the Cousin who could be a Great Friend, the Cousin who could know everything that Mona knew."

___12. "She had to grow fast and grow strong for Father. When the time came, Mother had to help her. She had to drink Mother's milk."

___13. "The Englishman, an affable man, a true Old World Gentleman it seemed, in a narrow seersucker suit . . . a man with the sharp melodious inflection of a British stage actor."

___14. "It was not her custom to speak into the phone when she answered it . . . if someone spoke, someone she knew, perhaps she would answer."

___15. "But all the basic ingredients of life are there—cellular structure most certainly, amino acids and DNA, and an organizing force that binds the whole regardless of its size and which responds now perfectly to the consciousness of the being which can reshape the entire entity at will."

___16. "[He] touched the tenderness in me, seducing me with his staggering dependence, his infatuation with my every gesture and every spoken word. And his naïveté conquered me always, his strange bourgeois faith that God was still God. . . ."

___17. "Of course it was the countryside that drew her, the forest or the mountains, or islands on which no human beings lived."

___18. "I couldn't stop myself from sensing a vast secret terrain inside him, grimmer perhaps than I had ever dreamed, and his words came back to me that the darkness in him was like the darkness I'd seen at the inn, and that he tried to conceal it from me."

___19. "She was kissing me, kissing the artery through which her own blood so violently flowed. Her lips were opening on it, and I drew on her blood with all my strength . . . I felt the unmistakable sensation of her fangs going into my neck."

___20. "He wore long trousers and old-fashioned

131

button shoes, polished to a perfect luster. As he smiled, his gently lined face with its curling white hair and blue eyes seemed to grow ever more vivid."

___21. "She had long blue-jean legs and wavy blond pageboy hair blowing softly against the hollow of her cheek. Young and fresh she looked, and effortlessly seductive in a tightly fitted and tapering navy blue peacoat."

___22. "His skin was a mass of scars, a hideous covering of injured flesh, as though every wrinkle of his 'death' had left its mark upon him . . . and his once clear gray eyes were shot with hemorrhaged vessels."

___23. "For an uptown girl, it's sort of, you know, de rigueur to have a large vocabulary."

___24. "Perfectly monstrous suddenly—a man who was taller than an ordinary man. A slight figure but the perfect incarnation of menace with its blue eyes . . . mouth vivid beneath the black gleam of the mustache, white fingers long and bony. . . ."

___25. "[His] red hair had been matted and shaggy, and his face so deeply wrinkled that his eyes were no longer fully visible."

___26. "He fell into a trance in a darkened theater."

___27. ". . . no matter how great his loneliness, or how long the search for brothers and sisters in whom he might find some comfort, he never worked the Dark Trick himself."

___28. "You said you would suffer martyrdom; torments unspeakable . . . if only you were to be someone who was good."

___29. "[She] almost never moved from the television screen. . . . The others had all recovered from what had happened. . . . She'd been damaged in some crucial way before it all began."

___30. "[Her] headless body was sliding down the fractured glass wall, the shards still falling around it. Blood streamed down the broken glass behind her. And the woman held [her] severed head by the hair!"

Who Said What Bonus Questions

From the character list above, indicate whom the quote describes:

___ 1. "[She was a] challenging combination of the mundane and the mysterious."

___ 2. "Huge black eyes seeming to stretch the white flesh in deep folds, the nose long and thin, and the mouth the jester's smile. There were the fang teeth, just touching the colorless lip, and the hair, a gleaming mass of black and silver. . . ."

___ 3. "In many a country from India to Mexico, he passed for a native."

___ 4. "He was powerfully built, but he moved as if he were a thin, tentative creature."

___ 5. "To see the mild face of _____ disfigured with rage was a terrible thing to behold. This is what angels look like, thought Yuri, when they come with their flaming swords."

From the character list above, match the characters with their statements:

___ 1. "As I see it, there's weakness and there's strength. And there is good art and bad art. And that is what I believe in."

___ 2. "Ask for it . . . and you will live forever."

___ 3. "I have to forecast. I have to speak. I have to declare."

___ 4. "I'm what's called a high prole."

___ 5. "The moment I saw him, saw his extraordinary aura and knew him to be no creature I'd ever known, I was reduced to nothing."

PART II

Anne Rice:
Life and Writings

Although Anne Rice is best known for the novels that comprise her Dark Universe, she has written other books as well. The following chapters include questions about Rice herself and four of her historical and erotic novels.

CHAPTER ELEVEN

Anne Rice

The following questions were compiled from interviews, articles, and Prism of the Night: A Biography of Anne Rice, *as well as from information contributed by Anne Rice herself.*

Short Answer

1. When was Anne Rice born?
2. Where was she born?
3. What was her full birthname?
4. What was her confirmation name?
5. How many nicknames has she had?
6. How old was she when she moved to Texas?
7. How old was she when she met Stan Rice, who would become her husband?
8. What were the circumstances under which she met Stan Rice?

9. When did Anne and Stan get married?

10. When was their daughter, Michele, born?

11. When was their son, Christopher, born?

12. What was Rice's major at San Francisco State College?

13. Name Rice's most famous dog.

14. What is Rice's favorite color for clothing?

15. What is her shoe size, and what is her favorite style of shoe?

16. How many typewriters does Rice own?

17. Who bought her her first typewriter?

18. How does Rice celebrate movie sales?

19. What is her favorite chocolate bar?

20. What year did Rice start collecting dolls?

21. What was the first doll in her collection?

22. How many sisters does Rice have?

23. What does Rice consider the most romantic movie she has ever seen?

24. A seven-foot statue of what movie monster stands in Rice's office?

25. Who is Rice's favorite saint?

26. What was the most exciting Hollywood dinner event that Rice ever attended?

27. What is Rice's most recent obsession?

28. Why did Anne Rice buy the 47,000-square foot St. Elizabeth's orphanage in New Orleans?

29. How many houses have Rice and her husband owned?

30. Where is Rice's principal residence?

The Novels

Short Answer

1. Which novel did Anne Rice dedicate to herself?
2. Whose birthday does Claudia share?
3. Which two characters share Stan Rice's birthday?
4. What historical scenes delayed the writing of *The Witching Hour*?
5. What Gothic writers did Rice read to prepare for *The Witching Hour*?
6. One of Rice's former college teachers is a renowned expert on Dracula. Who is it?
7. Which vampire film most strongly influenced Rice's childhood ideas about vampires?
8. Louis's transformation into a vampire and his subsequent relationship with Lestat as his teacher was influenced by a popular author Rice read in the 1970s. Who was the author?
9. In the original version of *Interview with the Vampire*, Louis and Claudia meet other vampires in Paris who live in a mansion. What happens to Claudia?
10. *Interview with the Vampire* began as a short story. How many years later did Rice publish it as a novel?
11. What unusual clause appears in all of Rice's film contracts?

12. What was the subject of Rice's first novella, written in junior high?

13. Which New Orleans cemetery did Rice often walk through and play in as a child? (Hint: Lestat hides his valuables there.)

14. Lestat checked into Rice's favorite hotel. Name it.

15. Rice based the ambition of Lestat and Nicolas to run off to Paris on an ambition she shared with her college roommate, Ginny Mathis. Where did they go together?

16. Rice's favorite animal appears in her vampire novels. What is it?

17. What was the inspiration for the pseudonym Anne Rampling?

18. What are the names of the Roquelaure novels?

19. Rice originally wanted Rutger Hauer to play Lestat in any film that was made of her vampire novels. What film was she watching when she decided this?

20. When she devised the plot for *The Queen of the Damned*, Rice was reacting against the cliché she saw in a film that portrayed evil as darkness. What film was it?

21. Who was the physician that assisted Rice with research for *Cry to Heaven*?

22. Rice used her husband's poetry in some of her novels. What else does he do?

23. What line in *Interview with the Vampire* did Rice

142

have to ignore in order to write *The Vampire Lestat*?

24. Why did Rice make Lestat a rock star?

25. Which of her novels did Rice perceive as a structural failure?

26. Who was the gay activist and writer of pornography that befriended Rice and almost wrote a novel with her?

27. What two famous crime writers did Rice read in order to develop Lestat's voice?

28. What famous woman from New Orleans did Rice initially want to include in *The Feast of All Saints*?

29. What was the original first line of *Interview with the Vampire*?

30. What strange incident happened after Rice finished writing *Cry to Heaven*?

True or False

___ 1. Anne Rice lived in San Francisco before she married Stan.

___ 2. The human skull in Rice's office is real.

___ 3. The character of Lestat grew out of the character of Elliott in *Exit to Eden*.

___ 4. Rice wrote seven complete novels while living in San Francisco's Castro District.

___ 5. Rice's master's thesis was called *Nicholas and Jean*.

___ 6. Rice wrote *Interview with the Vampire* in five months.

___ 7. In an article for *Vogue*, Rice described her ideas about gender and androgyny by analyzing Mick Jagger's appeal.

___ 8. Rice's first publication was a short story.

___ 9. Anne Rice actually went to the girls' boarding school known as St. Rose de Limas that she described in *The Witching Hour*.

___10. Rice met her first agent, Phylliss Seidel, at a writers' conference.

___11. Vicky Wilson was Rice's first editor.

___12. The first novel in which Rice wrote from the first-person female perspective was *The Queen of the Damned*.

___13. The hardcover advance for *Interview with the Vampire* was $12,000.

___14. Paramount bought the film rights for *The Vampire Lestat*.

___15. Rice once wanted to write a novel about male ballet dancers.

___16. *The Mummy* was written initially as a television miniseries.

___17. Rice sent Michael Curry to Redemptorist, the same Catholic school she attended.

___18. When Rice was growing up, her older sister, Alice, was the person who most strongly supported Rice's writing efforts.

___19. Rice's favorite form of massage is accupressure.

___20. Rice published five novels between *Interview with the Vampire* and *The Vampire Lestat*.

Multiple Choice
Which of the following characters is influenced by the specific biographical trait or experience?

___ 1. The year Anne Rice spent at Texas Woman's University:

A) Deirdre Mayfair

B) Dolly Rose

C) Belinda

D) Rowan Mayfair

E) Michael Curry

___ 2. Anne Rice's doll collection:

A) Jeremy Walker   D) Antha Mayfair

B) Juliet Mercier   E) Marguerite Mayfair

C) Louis

___ 3. As a girl, Rice wanted desperately to learn the violin. She gives the ability she desired to

A) Lestat   D) Nicolas de Lenfent

B) Akasha   E) Guido Maffeo

C) Louis

___ 4. In college, Anne Rice realized that she was most strongly attracted to teachers who had enthusiasm for life and who could be real mentors. She gives this awareness to

A) Belinda Blanchard   D) Julie Stratford

B) Marcel St. Marie   E) Eric

C) Elliott Slater

___ 5. Anne Rice's childhood fear of a movie monster inspired

A) *Interview with the Vampire*

B) *Lasher*

C) *The Mummy*

D) *The Witching Hour*

E) *The Queen of the Damned*

__ 6. Anne Rice's love of Jack Kerouac's *On the Road* is shared by
A) Elliott Slater
B) Lestat
C) Jeremy Walker
D) Michael Curry
E) Belinda Blanchard

__ 7. During college, Rice went through a long spell of being terrified of death. She called this experience the Dark Moment, and she gave the same fear to
A) Nicolas de Lenfent
B) Claudia
C) Richard Lermontant
D) Carlo Treschi
E) Lestat

__ 8. As a child, Rice went through a religious phase. She spent hours in prayer and meditation in an oratory, which later showed up as the place where
A) Lestat read books
B) Louis hid his coffin
C) Dolly Rose did penance
D) Tonio practiced his singing
E) Claudia hid her diary

___ 9. Other writers in San Francisco questioned why Rice wrote about old houses in New Orleans. The same question is asked of
A) Antha Mayfair
B) Michael Curry
C) Lestat
D) Marcel St. Marie
E) Elliott Slater

___10. Once, in Anne Rice's childhood, she discovered that she was wearing two unmatched shoes. She was mortified and thought that anyone who noticed would think she was insane. She uses this experience to develop background for
A) Marie St. Marie
B) Carlotta Mayfair
C) Lisa Kelly
D) Deirdre Mayfair
E) Mary Jane Mayfair

___11. Anne learned to play chess by reading a book borrowed from the library. She gives this experience to
A) Augustin Mayfair
B) Sister Bridget Marie
C) Bonnie Blanchard
D) Christophe Mercier
E) Michael Curry

___12. Anne's mother loved movies and took her children to see them as often as possible. As a result, Anne saw many foreign films. Which of her characters reports the same experience?

A) Jeremy Walker
B) Antha Mayfair
C) Michael Curry
D) David Talbot
E) Yuri Stefano

___13. Raised Catholic, and feeling a deep affinity with the saints, Anne hoped one day to experience the stigmata. She didn't, but one of her characters does:

A) Lestat
B) Armand
C) Gretchen
D) Tonio Treschi
E) Cardinal Calvino

___14. For many years, Rice has kept personal diaries. She describes this practice via

A) Louis
B) Maharet
C) Aaron Lightner
D) Jean Jacques, the cabinetmaker
E) Ashlar

___15. As of this writing, Rice has been to each of the following settings for her novels except
A) Haiti
B) Scotland
C) Barbados
D) Glastonbury
E) Venice

___16. Rice purchased a gun and took shooting lessons. She gives this experience to
A) Mary Jane Mayfair
B) Mona Mayfair
C) Lestat
D) Jeremy Walker
E) Rowan Mayfair

___17. The Mayfair family has an unusual custom that Rice and her own family practiced. It is
A) Wearing only black
B) Watching foreign films
C) Speaking to the dead
D) Holding seances
E) Collecting antique dolls

___18. Rice uses her own houses as settings. The houses she mentions that she actually owned include those at all of the following locations except

A) Amelia Street
B) Seventeenth Street
C) First Street
D) Napoleon
E) Rue St. Ann

___19. The character who has a strongly Catholic father similar to Rice's is

A) Lisa Kelly
B) Belinda Blanchard
C) Marcel St. Marie
D) Tonio Treschi
E) Elliott Slater

___20. Rice once owned a house in Seven Points, Texas. She used her experience there to describe the background of

A) George Gallagher
B) Killer
C) Richard Lermontant
D) Baby Jenks
E) Jesse

Anne Rice Bonus Questions

1. How many times has Anne Rice seen a heavy snowfall in New Orleans, and how does she use this experience in her writing?
2. What does Anne Rice wear to bed?
3. Rice's daughter, Michele, influenced the physical description of Claudia. There is another character in Rice's fiction whose illness and subsequent death echoes Michele's tragic fate. Who is this character?
4. What shocking act did Anne Rice perform at her father's wake?
5. What does Anne Rice like to snack on when she is writing?

CHAPTER TWELVE

The Historical Novels of Anne Rice

The Feast of All Saints

Short Answer

1. What was Marcel St. Marie's racial heritage?
2. Whom did Marcel wish to emulate?
3. Why did Marcel's mother, Cecile, dislike his sister?
4. From what country did Marcel's mother come?
5. How many *gens de couleur libre* were estimated to live in New Orleans in the 1840s?
6. When is the Feast of All Saints?
7. What did *passe blanc* mean to free people of color?
8. After Jean Jacques died and left his writings to Marcel, what became of them?

9. Marcel's house was located on which street in the French Quarter?

10. Just outside the cottage where Marcel's mother and sister resided was an outbuilding that he used. What is its French name?

11. Before he met Christophe, what occupied Marcel each afternoon at Madame Lelaud's?

12. Whose private academy did Marcel attend before he went to Christophe's school?

13. Christophe returned to New Orleans from where?

14. When Madame Lelaud asked Christophe his name, he used an alias. Another character in one of Rice's novels used the same name. What is it?

15. What was the title of Christophe's novel?

16. Which character in Christophe's novel killed Charlotte?

17. What news did Michael Larson-Roberts deliver to Christophe about his novel?

18. In which hotel was Michael Larson-Roberts staying when he contracted yellow fever?

19. How many students attended the first day of Christophe's class?

20. How tall was Richard Lermontant's grandfather, Jean Baptiste?

21. What did Dolly Rose's daughter, Lisa, die of?

22. What did Dolly Rose charge Christophe for her slave Bubbles?

23. When the daguerreotype was introduced in

France, a free man of color brought it to New Orleans. What was his name?

24. Who was Philippe Ferronaire?

25. Who was Philippe's notary?

26. *Bontemps*, Philippe's plantation, was in which Louisiana parish?

27. When Philippe arrived at the cottage, he brought a book for Marcel. What was the subject of the book?

28. Philippe referred to Juliet Mercier by the name of a character out of Shakespeare. Who was the character?

29. What did Philippe give to his daughter, Marie, that later caused him trouble?

30. What was the custom known as *plaçage*?

Fill in the Blank

1. The classic novel that Anna Bella read to Marcel was _____.

2. Narcisse, a sculptor, made the statue for the grave of Dolly Rose's child. His ambition was to study in _____.

3. Before Marcel left for the Cane River Country, Christophe gave him _____.

4. The name of Tante Josette's plantation was *Sans Souci*, which means _____.

5. Marcel visited the church of _____ in the Cane River Country.

6. Marcel was at *Sans Souci* for _____ months.

7. Marcel's relatives in the Cane River area wanted him to marry _____, his cousin.

8. The law that required women of color to wear plain head coverings was called _____.

9. Marie's birthday, the Feast of the Assumption of the Virgin Mary, is on _____.

10. Captain _____, Dolly Rose's white lover, posed a threat to Christophe.

True or False

__ 1. Anna Bella's lover was Vincent Dazincourt.

__ 2. Vincent fought a duel on Christophe's behalf.

__ 3. Juliet Mercier was considered crazy.

__ 4. Richard Lermontant's father devised the plan to send Marie and Richard to Europe.

__ 5. Dolly Rose opened a whorehouse.

__ 6. Lisette was Philippe's daughter by a slave.

__ 7. Lisette took Marie to Dolly Rose's, where Marie was ruined.

__ 8. Cecile asked her daughter to go to the quadroon balls on Marcel's behalf.

__ 9. Marcel decided to take up the undertaker's trade.

__10. Philippe died in Cecile's bed.

Cry to Heaven

Fill in the Blank

1. Guido Maffeo was _____ years old when he was castrated.
2. Guido was from the town of _____.
3. Guido was _____ years old when he was scheduled to sing in his first opera in Rome before he lost his voice.
4. When Guido lost his voice, he went to the town of _____ to try to take his life.
5. Andre Treschi's title was _____.
6. Tonio's full name was _____.
7. Tonio Treschi's childhood nurse was _____
   _____.
8. Carlo was Tonio's _____.
9. Tonio first knew about Carlo from a strange impression in a _____.
10. _____ said to Tonio, "You are my immortality."
11. The phrase *evviva il coltello* means _____.
12. The mask that Tonio wore at his first carnival was called a _____.
13. Tonio first heard about great castrated singers from Alessandro. He saw one of them, and this same singer showed up at the debut performance that Tonio gave years later at the house of the

Contessa Lamberti. This singer's name was ___

___.

14. The Treschi country villa was located on the ___ River.

15. In the Treschi household, Guiseppe's function was as ___.

Short Answer

1. Who was the first castrato that Tonio encountered?

2. Who was Bettina Sanfredo?

3. What did Tonio's singing symbolize for Guido?

4. How did Beppo, Tonio's childhood tutor, die?

5. What was the full name of the place Tonio went for voice training after becoming a castrato?

6. Where did Guido pick up Paolo?

7. The maestro compared Tonio's voice to that of a supernatural creature. What creature was it?

8. What natural formation inspired and transformed Tonio after he arrived in Naples?

9. How long did Tonio remain at the conservatorio in Naples before he was initially dismissed?

10. What was Domenico's stage name?

11. What is the "greatest of all strengths" that Cardinal Calvino defined for Tonio?

12. After Marianna died, what did Tonio receive from Venice?

13. What was Signora Bianchi's relation to Tonio?

14. What was the name of Tonio's and Guido's favorite wine?

15. What amount of money was paid to hire Tonio for the opera in Rome?

16. Tonio's stage debut in Rome took place in what theater?

17. What was *Achille en Sciro*?

18. Tonio was compared to a mythical figure from Greek mythology. The same figure was used to describe Armand and Gabrielle. Who was it?

19. Where did Tonio meet the Count Raffaele di Stefano?

20. What service did the Count perform for him?

21. Before Tonio's first performance in Rome, his detractors devised a nickname for him, *La ragazzina*. What does it mean?

22. What was Cardinal Calvino's relationship to Contessa Lamberti?

23. What was Christina Grimaldi's occupation?

24. During which religious season did Tonio arrive in Venice to confront his father?

25. Which of the following characteristics is *not* associated with a eunuch? (a) above-average height (b) flexible bones (c) flat feet (d) long arms (e) large eyes

Historical Fiction Bonus Questions

1. What was the significance for Rice of the title *The Feast of All Saints*?

2. How old was Richard's sister, Françoise, when she died?

3. Christophe quoted St. Augustine early in *The Feast of All Saints*, setting up the theme. What was the quote?

4. What newspaper did the *gens* read in 1840s New Orleans?

5. Which New Orleans cemetery was reserved for Protestants?

6. When Rice wrote *Cry to Heaven*, she listened to the only castrato whose voice was ever recorded. Name him.

7. Which scene in *Cry to Heaven* was written to music?

8. What book represented nobility and immortality to the Venetian nobility?

9. When Tonio cried out against Cardinal Calvino's rejection, he compared himself to a mythical Greek figure, "a wretched creature whose limbs had the unfortunate conformation of an object of desire." Name this figure.

10. To what mythical place did Guido compare Naples?

CHAPTER THIRTEEN

The Erotica
of Anne Rampling

Exit to Eden

Fill in the Blank

1. Lisa's nickname was _____.
2. Lisa was _____ tall.
3. Lisa was from _____, California.
4. The name of Lisa's female attendant was _____
   _____.
5. The Club's newspaper, which Lisa supervised,
   was _____.
6. Lisa compared The Club to the mythical place
   of _____.
7. _____ was The Club's principal finan-
   cier.
8. The ship that brought Elliott to The Club was the
   _____.

9. Elliott made a connection with Lisa before he even met her by watching one of her favorite movies, _____, while he was on his way to the island.

10. Elliott smokes _____ cigarettes.

Short Answer

1. What type of gin does Lisa drink?
2. How many rooms were in The House, where Lisa trained?
3. What is Elliott's graduate degree?
4. Which of Elliott's two books did he give to Lisa?
5. What message did he put into this book for Lisa?
6. How old was Richard, the youngest chief administrator at The Club?
7. What is the annual top membership fee at The Club?
8. Lisa wanted to put a train on the grounds of The Club. What was her name for it?
9. How many members were at The Club when Elliott first arrived?
10. Lisa was frightened by a Louisiana roach. What is the other name for this bug?
11. What kind of perfume was Lisa wearing when she first approached Elliott?
12. Where did Lisa and Elliott go when they left Louisiana?

13. Where did they go dancing?

14. In Texas, Lisa and Elliott jokingly referred to themselves as what infamous couple?

15. Who came to New Orleans to ask Michael and Lisa to return to The Club?

16. What is the location of the cottage in the French Quarter that Lisa rented?

17. Martin Halifax used a short story about a traveling salesman to show Lisa that she was in love and did not recognize it. Who wrote the story?

18. When Lisa planned to take Elliott to Venice, she booked a suite facing the lagoon. Name the suite.

19. Where did Elliott ask Lisa to marry him?

20. Where did Elliott suggest they get married?

Multiple Choice

___ 1. Near what large city was the meeting held to discuss The Club's design and execution?

A) New York

B) Los Angeles

C) Paris

D) Rome

E) Mexico City

__ 2. Name the song heard near the small cottage that Lisa rented in the French Quarter for Elliott and herself:

A) "Running on Empty"

B) "Violetta's Waltz"

C) "If You Could Read My Mind"

D) "Beat It"

E) "Ruby Tuesday"

__ 3. Name the first restaurant in New Orleans where Elliott and Lisa ate together:

A) Manale's   D) Caribbean Room

B) Galatoire's   E) Commander's Palace

C) Café du Monde

__ 4. Elliott and Lisa stopped in a motel in a town outside New Orleans that also figures in *Lives of the Mayfair Witches*. What town is it?

A) Metairie   D) Destin

B) Napoleonville   E) La Place

C) St. Martinville

__ 5. Elliott and Lisa had their first fight over how to interpret a movie. Name the movie they discussed:

A) *Alien*   D) *Flashdance*

B) *Pretty Baby*   E) *Captain Blood*

C) *Angelo, My Love*

___ 6. Who was Lisa's favorite male attendant at
    The Club?
A) Scott   D) Daniel
B) Richard   E) Elliott
C) Michael

___ 7. What was Scott's nickname?
A) the Panther   D) the Rebel
B) the Wolf   E) the Lover
C) the Prince

___ 8. A two-year contract for slaves at The Club
    pays
A) $50,000
B) $100,000
C) $200,000
D) $350,000
E) Nothing; the slaves pay for the privilege of be-
    ing there

___ 9. Lisa went to a giant flea market in Canton,
    Texas, to look for
A) Porcelain dolls
B) Quilts
C) Sandals
D) Cowboy boots
E) Cowboy hats

—10. After The Club proved to be highly success-
ful, several imitators were established around
the world. Which is *not* mentioned as the location of one of them?

A) Holland
B) California
C) Copenhagen
D) Venice

Belinda

Short Answer

1. What was Belinda wearing when Jeremy first
saw her?
2. What did Belinda ask Jeremy to promise, on
threat of her leaving?
3. What was the occupation of Jeremy's late
mother?
4. Jeremy wrote two books in his mother's name
after she died. Ollie Boon was interested in one
of them for a movie. Which one?
5. What was the name of Jeremy's publicist?
6. What brand of cigarettes did Belinda smoke?
7. On what unusual type of bed did Jeremy sleep?
8. How many times has Jeremy been married?
9. Where was Belinda's room in San Francisco
before she moved in with Jeremy?

10. What kind of car did Jeremy drive?

11. When Belinda braided her hair to pose for pictures, Jeremy called her by the name of a character from literature. Who was it?

12. What alias did Belinda use when she ran away from Bonnie?

13. What kind of artist was Jeremy?

14. What was the name of Jeremy's artist friend from whom he bought a sculpture?

15. Ollie Boon staged a musical on Broadway that is named for a character in one of Rice's earliest novels. What was it?

16. How many full-panel paintings did Jeremy paint of Belinda?

17. Who was Count Solosky?

18. What item of clothing was the dark-haired Italian reporter wearing that gave her away as Belinda in disguise?

19. Both Bonnie and Belinda posed many years apart in an ad for the same product. What was it?

20. What was Bonnie's trademark?

21. What were featured in the darker paintings that Jeremy hid in his attic before he met Belinda?

22. What was the prime-time television show that revived Bonnie's career?

23. To whom did Blair refer as "the Gruesome Statistic"?

24. Where was G.G's house, in which Belinda stayed when she first ran away from Bonnie?

25. Where did Bonnie and Marty claim they had sent Belinda to school after she ran away?

26. On what street was Jeremy's mother's house located in New Orleans?

27. What actual house was it based on?

28. How many years older than Belinda was Jeremy?

29. What was the title of the first picture Jeremy painted of Belinda?

30. When Jeremy painted *Belinda with Dolls*, he gave her a doll from his collection. It is the same doll Rice gave to Ashlar, the Taltos. The doll is referred to by the name of its maker. What is it?

Fill in the Blank

1. On her nighttime soap opera, Bonnie played a character named _____.

2. Jeremy used the alias _____ when he tried to get information about Belinda from the publisher of Bonnie's biography.

3. Belinda stayed at the _____ Hotel when she first arrived in New York to find her father.

4. Belinda's birthday was on _____.

5. After Belinda left Jeremy, Susan Jeremiah first found evidence of her whereabouts in the city of _____.

6. When Jeremy first saw Belinda, he called her
_____.

7. Belinda also called Jeremy by the name of a character in a fairy tale: _____.

8. Belinda's father, G.G., had a secret name for her, _____, which he revealed to Alex Clementine.

9. Susan Jeremiah and Bonnie Blanchard were both from the state of _____.

10. Jeremy's house was located on _____ Street.

11. After G.G. was forced to close up his hairdressing business in New York, he decided to set up shop on _____.

12. The author's party at which Jeremy learned

Belinda's name was held in the _____
Hotel.

13. The last children's book that Jeremy wrote and
    illustrated was _____.

14. Jeremy had written _____ books in the
    series that features this character.

15. Altogether, Jeremy had written _____
    children's books.

16. The housekeeper in Jeremy's mother's house in
    New Orleans was _____._____.

17. Jeremy's secret California hideaway was in ____
    _____.

18. Belinda appeared without credit in as many
    as _____ films.

19. The first film in which she received credit was
    _____.

20. Blair's name for Jeremy was _____.

Anne Rampling Bonus Questions

1. Martin Halifax smoked a pipe. What brand of tobacco did he use?
2. In Elliott's cabin, there were two books by A. N. Roquelaure, another Rice pseudonym. Why wasn't the third one there?
3. Under what fictional name did Jean Paul advertise his place in San Francisco?
4. Lisa compared Elliott to an explorer. Name the explorer.
5. What film did Elliott watch, which he was "nuts" about, just before Lisa returned from New Orleans to The Club to admit her feelings to him?
6. What happened to Jeremy's father?
7. Where did Jeremy keep the keys to the attic room where he stored the paintings?
8. What was Alex Clementine's favorite meal?
9. At what San Francisco hotel did Jeremy meet Blair?
10. What was Bonnie's major in college, which earned her the reputation of being "nouvelle vague"?

PART III

Super Bonus
Questions

And you thought the preceding questions were hard.
Just wait until you turn the page!

Super Bonus Questions

Matching
Match the physicians with their patients:

___ 1. D. Anelle Salter   A. Rowan Mayfair

___ 2. Dr. Jack   B. Michael Curry

___ 3. Dr. Fitzroy   C. Mona Mayfair

___ 4. Dr. Fleming   D. Morrigan Mayfair

___ 5. Dr. Larry Petrie   E. Mary Beth Mayfair

___ 6. Dr. Lyndon Hart   F. Antha Mayfair

___ 7. Dr. Morris   G. Deirdre Mayfair

___ 8. Dr. Rhodes   H. Ancient Evelyn

Match the First Street help with the jobs they performed for the Mayfairs:

___ 1. Viola   A. Cook

___ 2. Henri   B. Michael's first chauffeur

___ 3. Yancy   C. General maintenance

___ 4. Bertha Marie Becker   D. Michael's construction foreman

___ 5. Alice Flanagan   E. Infant Deirdre's nurse

___ 6. Maria Magdalene Gabrielli   F. Mowed the lawn, despite Lasher

___ 7. Irene   G. Antha's first nurse

___ 8. Dart Henley   H. Antha's second nurse

___ 9. Miss Lampton   I. Mary Beth's secretary

___10. Alain Mayfair   J. Deirdre's tutor

___11. Ronnie   K. Maid for Carlotta and Antha

___12. Eugenia   L. Maid for Mary Beth

___13. Patricia Devlin   M. Recent chauffeur

___14. Cullen   N. Maid for Carlotta, then Michael

___15. Aunt Easter   O. Nurse for the comatose Deirdre

___16. Christian   P. Julien's manservant

1. Who was Dr. Lemle's secretary at the Keplinger Institute?
2. Benjy was the name of the Cajun boy who helped Granny Mayfair, but it was also the name of a character mentioned in *The Witching Hour*. Who is the other Benjy?
3. What was Dr. Jack's wife's name?
4. Who was Marie Louise Guidry?
5. What position did Hercules have with the Mayfairs?
6. The Comte de Montcleve was a member of what religious group?
7. What were the names of Marguerite's two quadroon servants?
8. What was Octavius's relationship to the Mayfair family?
9. Which Talamasca member discovered a source of Mayfair gossip in Irwin Dandrich?
10. Who was Ona Patrick?
11. What was Judith's nickname for Michael Curry?
12. What novel did Michael read after Rowan left him and fled with Lasher?
13. Where was Baby Jenks from originally?
14. Who was David Talbot's young lover in Brazil?
15. Which vampire in Armand's coven was jealous of Claudia's beauty?

16. During the feast that preceded the attack on the tribe of the twins, Khayman passed something to Enkil and Akasha. What was it?

17. What did Louis sign over to Lestat before he prepared to leave New Orleans with Claudia?

18. What color were Daniel's eyes?

19. What was the name of the mortal boy whom Armand gave to Louis for a brief drink of blood?

20. What was the name of the ship on which Louis and Claudia sailed to Eastern Europe?

21. What was the fate of the golden locket that contained a miniature painting of Claudia?

22. Lestat saved the paintings of what artist when he burned down Louis's Uptown mansion?

23. Where did Akasha live before she became queen of Kemet?

24. Who was the parking attendant at the Talamasca Motherhouse in London?

25. At Maye Faire, what was Reginald's function?

26. Who gave Michael Curry the black gloves that he wore?

27. Who was the Comte de Montcleve's mistress?

28. Who was the groupie that followed Lestat's rock band from New Orleans to San Francisco?

29. What did Louis produce on his plantation?

30. Whom did Petyr van Abel first consult in Amsterdam to locate the runaway Deborah?

31. Who was Jeanne Angelique de Roulet?

32. What kind of gun does Anne Rice own?

33. In what film did Anne Rice's dog, Sonny, appear?

34. How many girls could live in the former orphanage that Anne Rice recently purchased?

35. What is Anne Rice's most secret playful fantasy?

True or False

___ 1. On the genealogies that Julien examines in Edinburgh, Ranald is listed as Janet's father.

___ 2. Scott Reynolds replaced David Talbot as Talamasca director.

___ 3. Petyr van Abel thinks Roelant's artistic style is like that of Botticelli.

___ 4. Lestat murdered a serial killer known as the Miami Menace.

___ 5. Yuri was ten years old when he first met Aaron Lightner.

___ 6. Graham Franklin's first boat was the *Great Angela*.

___ 7. Louis hears the "Pange Lingua" before he has visions of Lestat's funeral procession.

___ 8. The constellation honored by the twin witches Mekare and Maharet and seen by Daniel as he was being made a vampire is Orion.

___ 9. Those Who Must Be Kept were once protected by Marius on Pompeii.

___10. The first album recorded by Lestat's rock group sold one million copies.

___11. Marius called Lestat Prince Charming.

___12. Marty Moreschi's sign is Scorpio.

___13. Julie Stratford's room number at the hotel in Cairo is 302.

___14. Fifteen people died from Lasher's attack on Montcleve.

___15. Deirdre Mayfair was born at Touro Medical Center.

PART IV

Answers

Answers

Chapter One
The Savage Garden: Night Creatures and Dark Powers

What Lurks in the Dark Universe: An Overview

Short Answer

1. The Savage Garden is another name for nature, but a nature that embraces such monsters as vampires.
2. Aesthetic principles; only beauty is consistent.
3. Santino's coven.
4. Ancient vampires, such as Marius, Pandora, and Mael. They are considered outlaws by the Roman coven.

5. The fingernails are highly polished and look like glass.
6. The Dark Gift is the power to become immortal. That power is conveyed by the working of the Dark Trick, through which mortals are transformed into vampires.
7. The Devil's Road.
8. The queen vampire in Armand's coven.
9. The Devil.
10. A succubus.
11. The tribe ate them; cannibalism was a spiritual activity.
12. Candomble.
13. The residual soul. (The higher or astral soul is the other part.)
14. The sun.
15. Reincarnation.
16. Of dipping their torches in the fat of unbaptized children.
17. Throwing live Taltos onto the burning log for sacrifice.
18. He killed four women merely by having sex with them.
19. The giant helix, or "the double dose of the double helix."
20. The bell the priests rang to scare away demons, particularly the Little People.
21. Their cells die in intense heat or cold, and their enzymes dissolve the residue.

22. People of Peace.

23. Aiken Drumm.

24. The theories about the Little People include the following: They may be angels caught between heaven and hell; they are the spawn of a pair of Wild Taltos; they are the result of a Taltos's failure to get enough milk; they are the halfbreed spawn of a witch and a Taltos; they are the runtish offspring of Taltos that failed to grow during a prehistoric period. For now, their true origin remains a mystery.

25. Loch Ness and Glamis Castle.

True or False

1. T   2. T   3. T   4. F: It is another name for the Little People.   5. F: He thought that Taltos have two lives and that Tessa was a reincarnated Taltos. 6. T 7. F: The ghost's mother was a prostitute, not the girl, Antoinette.   8. T   9. T   10. F: He was considered the First Street ghost.   11. F: He was possessed for ten years.   12. F: His book was *Demonologie*. 13. T   14. F: Ghosts can be vindictive, she says, but are mostly impotent and irrelevant.   15. T.

The Spirit World: Ghosts and Discarnate Entities

Short Answer

1. Ghosts once had bodies, although spirits can act like ghosts.
2. They have a tiny physical core and the same DNA as humans.
3. It pierces the cellular structure, fuses with the cells, and transforms the human tissue into a substance similar to itself but lighter, and more solid and dense.
4. A spirit becomes aware of itself via some human's awareness of it.
5. Stuart Townsend's.
6. He must focus on pattern, so Julien picked a piece of music from *La Traviata*.
7. A mansion in New York designed by architect Stanford White that no longer exists. (She also saw Claudia, the ghost of a vampire).
8. Miriam, her deceased mother.
9. It has twice the number of chromosomes in human DNA—92.
10. After Jesse found Claudia's diary in the town house.
11. That it was a projection of his conscience; he felt guilty about making her a vampire.

12. His dead brother, Paul, who was said to haunt the spot where he fell to his death.
13. The inhabitants of a house with a tower, which he and Louis climbed in Paris.
14. Red hair and green eyes.
15. They can spread a destructive religion by pretending to be the gods.
16. The heart.
17. The cells of the corpse are no longer dividing and renewing themselves, so spirits cannot organize the cells according to their will.
18. That humans are a mixture of flesh and spirit.
19. That humans possess a mind like the spirits but also feel the pleasures of the flesh.
20. Although he was merely spirit, he managed to prick her skin and draw blood.

Lasher

Short Answer

1. A pentagram.
2. Over a century, from 1559 to 1665.
3. As a Scotsman in a leather jerkin.
4. At 3:05 A.M., the moment Deirdre died.
5. The Man.
6. That he was getting stronger and appearing more often.

7. Antoine Père Fontenay.

8. A loud band playing incessant music; it both attracted and distracted him.

9. *The Queen of the Damned.*

10. Douglas of Donnelaith.

11. Saint Ashlar.

12. Assisi, Italy, with the Franciscans.

13. In the circle of stones.

14. He promised to bring them back into the flesh and make them immortal, if they would first do the same for him.

15. Chase, her former boyfriend.

16. When Petyr van Abel pushed Father Louvier to his death.

17. Lucrezia.

18. The fontanel remained soft.

19. The missing Mayfair emerald.

20. Beneath Deirdre's oak.

Multiple Choice

1. E (It is Amel who pricks the skin.) 2. E 3. D (It was Julien's idea to allow Lasher to possess him, for self-preservation.) 4. B 5. C 6. A, C, D, F, H, I, J, L, N, P, R, S

Taltos

Fill in the Blank

1. three   2. Wild Taltos   3. brochs   4. walking baby
5. Picts   6. Ogham   7. India   8. Glastonbury Abbey
9. Jerome   10. milk

Short Answer

1. Rice took it from Hungarian folklore, in which a *Taltos* was a type of witch.
2. They tricked him with the illusion that one of their women was a Taltos.
3. They vowed to become celibate.
4. Dancing to music and getting caught up to the point of entrapment.
5. The Antichrist.
6. He or she was sent to Britain, the land of Winter.
7. Janet offered Ashlar hope of absolution and regeneration of the race.
8. By the unusual eyes and the faint sheen on the skin.
9. They served as sentries during the birth ritual to prevent humans from seeing it.
10. That she would become one of the Little People.
11. His skeleton measured seven feet in length.
12. Simple People of the Stones or Fools of the Circle.

13. "Legends of the Lost Land: Of Stonehenge."
14. The Sacred Hunt.
15. She cursed the clan of Donnelaith, and in 1689, Lasher killed the last of the clan still in Donnelaith.
16. Chains of memories.
17. Art of the Tongue.
18. An infant Taltos being born.
19. On Glastonbury Tor.
20. Off the coast of Unst in Scotland.

Ashlar

True or False

1. T   2. F: It was because of his ability to make practical connections.   3. T   4. F: Ashlar befriended only Samuel; he barely tolerated Aiken Drumm.   5. T   6. F: It was King Olaf.   7. F: He commissioned her to make dolls that smiled.   8. T   9. T   10. T   11. T   12. F: He gave this history book to Ninian; he did not know how it ended up in the Talamasca archives where Stuart Gordon found it.   13. T   14. T   15. T   16. F: He sent Michael his book on the Taltos.   17. T   18. T   19. F: Stuart Gordon believed this; Ashlar denied it.   20. F: Samuel wanted a bulldog.

Short Answer

1. New York.
2. Leslie.
3. Remmick.
4. Belgravia.
5. *History of the Taltos of Britain: Giants in the Earth.*
6. The cave where he saw the vision of Janet.
7. Take care of Tessa and don't try to contact him.
8. Anton Marcus, for his part in the corruption.
9. The secret fax number for the Elders.
10. In the Trattoria dell'Arte on Seventh Avenue in New York.

Supernatural Powers

Multiple Choice

1. E 2. C 3. B 4. B 5. A 6. D 7. E 8. D 9. B 10. A

Short Answer

1. Landing Smith stole a large sum of money. Mary Beth magically appeared (via bilocation) on the ship Smith took and beat him; he consequently went mad.

2. The coins always return to the purse; it never empties.

3. He touched Deborah's portrait and predicted that Petyr van Abel would die and that the Mayfair history would be very dark.

4. Moving small objects with his mind (telekinesis).

5. The marker is possessing psychic powers.

6. He asked Lauren Grant, who had the power of psychometry, to touch an article of Deirdre's clothing. She tells him that Deirdre is blissful.

7. Cloaking.

8. The heightened perception that a vampire experiences; the ability to see everything from a new perspective and to deeply appreciate it.

9. They attracted spirits and induced them to make rain; they could also use the spirits to read the future and find lost objects.

10. Put someone into a trance.

The Mummy

Short Answer

1. Lawrence saw a writing table, several jars of poisons, a library of scrolls, and a mummy case without a sarcophagus.

2. Edwardian; 1914.

3. Seventeenth Earl of Rutherford, or Lord Rutherford.

4. "Morning Papers Waltz."

5. In a Cairo museum.

6. A hooker that Henry Stratford kept in London.

7. The Egyptian Room.

8. Viscount Summerfield.

9. Madame Tussaud's wax museum.

10. Ramses' son when he was a mortal king.

11. The Thomas Cook agency.

12. The colossal statues of Ramses II.

13. Ramses claimed that the dominant theme of modern times is change, while the dominant theme of ancient times, when he reigned, was that all things would remain the same.

14. The American heiress whom Alex met in Cairo. Elliott hoped Charlotte would consider marrying Alex.

15. The Grand Colonial Hotel.

16. In the catacombs in Alexandria, down a narrow passage that led to a secret room; his sleeping place was in a portal cut high up into the wall.

17. Zaki ran a mummy factory, where he embalmed and wrapped bodies to sell to English tourists who wanted to purchase a "genuine" mummy.

18. Take large steps and swing her arms naturally.

19. King Ptolemy, in the time of Alexander.

20. Ramses gave it to him.

Fill in the Blank

1. Cleopatra   2. sixty-four   3. Malenka   4. Shelley
5. Babylon   6. Oscar   7. the pyramid tomb of King
Kufu   8. Pernod   9. Lancia Theta   10. Mayfair

Savage Garden Bonus Questions

1. Burning flesh.
2. Steal their knapsacks.
3. Twenty.
4. That he could learn.
5. On the trunk of the crepe myrtle at First Street.
6. It included his childhood fears of nuns and the Comus Parade.
7. To study vampires.
8. The addlebrained dead.
9. The mummified corpse of Khayman's father.
10. A silver bracelet.

Chapter Two
Vampires: The Children of the Night

Multiple Choice

1. D 2. E 3. D 4. A 5. E 6. C 7. B 8. E
9. C 10. A

Match the killing style:

1. D 2. B 3. E 4. A 5. C

Match the ages:

1. C 2. F 3. J 4. D 5. E 6. A 7. I 8. H
9. B 10. G

Short Answer

1. About 400 years old.
2. That if she cut her hair, it would grow back to the length it was when she became a vampire; she wants to cut it short and cannot.
3. The aging vampire's need for blood diminishes, but some still drink blood just because they like it.
4. Azim.
5. It was part of the boy reporter's unpublished tapes of Louis's confession.

6. The repeated question "Do you love me?" seems to be asked by the women, but in fact it is asked by Armand.

7. Going Underground.

8. Maharet's eyes were torn out before she became a vampire, so she borrowed mortals' eyes, which wear out and see things only dimly.

9. He wanted to avoid the Plague.

10. She transferred the title from her brother's name to her own, thereby legally circumventing her father's final instructions that Richard destroy it.

11. In 1888, the year of Jack the Ripper.

12. Amadeo, which means "one who loves God."

13. Armand's blood.

14. Put a dagger in Akasha's heart to test the legend that Akasha was the source of the vampires' immortality.

15. Killing other vampires is exciting and so it was forbidden.

16. Many corpses of young blond men like himself, in various states of decay.

17. The Elder.

18. Four years.

19. At the Sonoma compound.

20. Five: Akasha, Enkil, Khayman, Mekare, and Maharet.

21. Santino.

22. She sleeps deep in the earth, usually in the woods.

23. He went back to the house on Divisadero Street; it seemed the safest place.

24. She was assigned to investigate the New Orleans town house where the vampires Lestat, Louis, and Claudia had once lived.

25. In Barbados.

26. Gabrielle.

27. Ninety-nine percent.

28. Human progress.

29. "Requiem for the Marquise."

30. Night Island.

Fill in the Blank

1. the Vampire Connection 2. Dead guy 3. sixty-five
4. saint 5. Dracula's Daughter 6. Calamity 7. violin
8. chrysanthemums 9. Queen Victoria 10. Evil
Eye 11. the presence 12. Azim 13. mummers
14. Emily 15. Pandora 16. gold chain 17. fifteen
18. Pandora 19. Armand 20. gold pocket watch
21. cemeteries 22. Nicolas 23. Venetian brothel 24. Feast of Samhain 25. Armand 26. Parker
27. coffin 28. wolves 29. Great Family 30. twentysix

The Dark Realm from Louis's Perspective

Short Answer

1. One, but he does not name the person.
2. Lestat wanted his plantation.
3. Help Lestat kill the overseer.
4. The oratory that he had built for his brother, Paul.
5. He said he had a malarial chill; he also "suffered from headaches."
6. Claustrophobia; he hated being shut into coffins, and in Paris he was nailed into one.
7. He slit the throat of a rat, drained the blood into a goblet, then drank it.
8. Lestat told Louis he would die along with the victim.
9. From victims whose names he knew; he would only drink from strangers.
10. Babette Freniere.
11. She thought he was the Devil and she died insane.
12. A white horse.
13. Old World vampires.
14. Louis.
15. In the Latin Quarter.
16. Dismemberment.
17. She claimed that Armand wanted her to die so he could have Louis to himself.

18. Armand induced Louis, against Louis's better judgment, to make Madeleine a vampire for Claudia.

19. A scythe.

20. The Louvre.

21. In Lestat's hideout in the Carmel Valley.

22. Gabrielle.

23. That Claudia's ghost had appeared to her there.

24. Purgatory.

25. That she should allow humans to evolve according to their own visions.

The Dark Realm from Lestat's Perspective

Short Answer

1. Louis reminded Lestat of Nicolas, so Lestat fell in love with him.

2. A rock group he met gave him the book *Interview with the Vampire* because they thought it was amusing that he called himself Lestat.

3. Satan's Night Out.

4. Absinthe and laudanum.

5. Once, on the stage in Renaud's theater. He was nearly shot on the *QE2*.

6. Christine.

7. He claimed to be married to an heiress from Saint-Domingue.

8. Pierre Roget.
9. His mother, Gabrielle.
10. Mastiffs.
11. Gretchen was the name of the girl that Faust seduced and ruined; the nun's name is in keeping with the Faustian theme of *The Tale of the Body Thief.*
12. Mojo.
13. Harley-Davidson.
14. Madame LeClair.
15. Twilight.
16. Velvet.
17. He acquired a great tan that allowed him to pass as a mortal.
18. Eight.
19. Jim Morrison; Baby Jenks thinks he sounds like Bruce Springsteen.
20. The Cow Palace in San Francisco.

Multiple Choice

1. C 2. B 3. A 4. A 5. E 6. C 7. B 8. C
9. D 10. E

Vampire Bonus Questions

1. The Nyades Road ghost.
2. White roses.
3. "Beware."
4. M. R. James's "Count Magnus."
5. Barbara.
6. First he placed it in his own crypt in the St. Louis cemetery; then he removed it, smashed it to pieces, and left it in the cemetery.
7. A radio.
8. An emerald ring.
9. Stealer of the Mother and Father.
10. An emerald rosary.

Chapter Three
Witches: The Mayfair File

Matching

1. Y   2. M   3. W   4. AA   5. X   6. G   7. Z   8. S
9. H   10. I   11. O   12. R   13. J   14. L   15. DD
16. P   17. N   18. U   19. Q   20. D   21. E   22. CC
23. BB   24. T   25. V   26. B   27. K   28. C   29. F
30. A

Fill in the Blank

1. Brazil   2. Rita Mae Dwyer   3. Lauren   4. Carondelet   5. pearls   6. ricin   7. pirogue   8. Stella
9. Mary Beth   10. Thorazine

Short Answer

1. Julien died in 1914 and Antha was born in 1921.
2. She tried to have it buried with Stella.
3. That Michael had performed his function—making Rowan pregnant.
4. Twelve years old.
5. Drummard.
6. Judge Fleming was her employer at Byrnes, Brown and Blake.
7. Four: Charlotte, Jeanne Louise, Angélique, and Marie Claudette.
8. Twenty, stored at First Street.
9. Katherine.
10. Charlotte was born too early to have been the Comte de Montcleve's child, which cast Deborah in a suspicious light.
11. She died in an enclosed room in which the gas had been left on.
12. She went dancing at the quadroon balls and pretended to be one of the quadroons; white men who danced with her there were outraged to discover the truth.

13. Her mother was unmarried and died at First Street after Nancy was born. Mary Beth raised Nancy as Stella's daughter.

14. La Victoire.

15. She would print words from the dictionary on pieces of paper, roll them into balls, put them into a hat, and extract them one at a time to learn them; whatever words seemed impractical, she'd toss out.

16. Four city blocks.

17. Her husband, Sean Lacy.

18. Peter's name is "Pierre" in Lasher's genealogy.

19. Stella believed that she needed thirteen Mayfair witches gathered in one spot to invoke Lasher and gain immortality from him; "the thirteen," in fact, meant thirteen generations of witches.

20. She was thought to be the daughter of the earl, so when he offered to give her a religious education, it seemed the best way to be rid of her.

21. The witchpricker searched Deborah for the Devil's Mark by pricking her with a pointed instrument to discover places that failed to bleed or seemed insensitive.

22. At her beach house in Destin, Florida.

23. Father Mattingly.

24. Fresh flowers appeared regularly after Stella died.

25. Darcy Monahan.

Multiple Choice

1. C 2. B 3. E 4. A 5. E 6. B 7. D 8. D
9. C 10. C

Julien Mayfair

True or False

1. T 2. T 3. F: He put them in the Victrola 4. T:
Richard Llewellyn 5. T 6. F: He appeared to Michael after the near-accident and urged him to go
home. 7. T 8. T 9. F: He appeared to her *before*
he died 10. T: he did this with Richard.

Short Answer

1. He asked her if she remembered something that
   he knew had never happened. When she pretended to remember, he knew the ghost was
   Lasher's invention.
2. From pink to violet.
3. The poem that predicted the demise of the Mayfairs because of their involvement with Lasher.
4. Jeannette.
5. They were his "good" self.
6. The vengeful spirit of a man named Ashlar.

7. The original pamphlet that detailed Suzanne's execution.
8. Julien's child with Sister Bridget Marie (although he later indicated that his child with her was female).
9. Gallatin Street.
10. "You have served your purpose."

Michael Curry

Short Answer

1. Michael James Timothy Curry.
2. Forty-eight.
3. In St. Alphonsus at Christmas and at a violin concert.
4. The Irish Channel.
5. Timothy Curry was a fire-fighter.
6. Isaac Stern.
7. *La Bohème.*
8. His fear of the Comus parade.
9. San Francisco State College (now University).
10. Elizabeth and Judith.
11. Aunt Vivian.
12. Gifford Mayfair; it was still in her purse when she died.
13. Porcelain Christmas ornaments.
14. Great Expectations.

15. Because Michael was "afraid of ghosts. . . . It's an Irish trait." *(LR 206)*
16. His heart, after nearly drowning twice and having several heart attacks.
17. At the Talamasca retreat at Oak Haven.
18. He wanted to go back on the boat that rescued him and put his hands on the deck so that he could recall a vision he believed he had had in the ocean. Rowan owned the boat.
19. He is the descendant of one of Julien's illegitimate children.
20. A hammer.

Multiple Choice

1. B   2. E   3. B   4. A   5. D

Rowan Mayfair

True or False

1. T   2. F: It is the *Sweet Christine*   3. T   4. T
5. T   6. F: He first spoke to her at Ellie's grave 7. F: She went to the University of California at Berkeley.
8. F: Rowan was repulsed by the experiments and decided against going into research medicine.   9. T
10. F: She knocked him out with the back of a toilet.   11. T.   12. F: He appeared at First Street   13. F:

206

She was glad she read it   14. F: Rowan killed Stuart
Gordon   15. T

Mona Mayfair

Fill in the Blank

1. Paige   2. Alicia   3. Deirdre's funeral   4. Yuri
Stefano   5. St. Alphonsus   6. Mayfair crypt   7. Fontevrault   8. Pierce   9. thirteen   10. Sacred Heart
Academy   11. Whore of Babylon   12. Julien's Victrola and Stella's pearls   13. sixth finger   14. flower
girl   15. Rowan

Witches Bonus Questions

1. Three Grady Mayfairs.
2. So that Antha could not look at Lasher and feed
   him with her attention.
3. She had bruises on her body.
4. Lestan Mayfair.
5. Philippe was older than Chrétien.
6. That he would haunt First Street with Lasher;
   they would be ghosts together.
7. Darius, King of Persia.
8. Pachelbel's *Canon*.

9. Boston.
10. Stutz Bearcat.

Chapter Four
The Experts: The Talamasca

Short Answer

1. They were both alchemists.
2. To make no judgment about paranormal phenomena, because the unknown is not necessarily evil.
3. The Dutchman who approached Lasher in the sixteenth century.
4. David Talbot.
5. Aaron Lightner.
6. Petyr van Abel.
7. As a Swiss Calvinist scholar.
8. He might have been an artist or a physician like his father.
9. He said they were the "active mode."
10. Deirdre Mayfair tried to give it to him, but he was afraid Lasher would kill him.
11. Lanzing, who was hired by Marklin George to "take care" of Yuri.
12. The Grand Design.
13. They shoved Marklin and Tommy into a pit in

the cellar and bricked them in, leaving them to
die.

14. Judith de Wilde, who lived with Deborah for
awhile.

15. *The Temptation of Amadeo*.

16. Khayman.

17. Latin.

18. A female Taltos.

19. The Order elected Stuart Gordon, but he passed
the position on to Joan Cross.

20. The Order told him not to approach Lestat and
not to be with him alone.

21. He saw Stella's murder.

22. Aaron Lightner tried to contact her to talk about
the Mayfair file.

23. Stella wrote a message to them on a photograph
that she knew was going to be sold to them.

24. Rice saw the word in a book on witchcraft by
Jeffrey Burton Russell.

25. A, B, E

Matching
Match the Talamasca informants:

1. K   2. H   3. F   4. L   5. E   6. I   7. C   8. D
9. B   10. J   11. A   12. G

Match the Talamasca members:

1. H   2. A   3. I   4. K   5. B   6. G   7. F   8. L
9. N   10. M   11. O   12. C   13. J   14. D   15. E

Multiple Choice

1. D   2. C   3. E   4. D   5. C   6. A   7. B   8. C
9. E   10. B

Talamasca Bonus Questions

1. On the canal, near or on the Singel gracht where Lestat sees David Talbot.
2. In the Talamasca cemetery in London.
3. The locket that contained a miniature of Claudia.
4. The New Delhi Motherhouse.
5. Twenty-three.
6. The Motherhouse in Rome.
7. Baron.
8. Scotch.
9. The London Motherhouse.
10. She saw Deirdre with Lasher at St. Rose de Lima's boarding school.

Chapter Five
Religion and Mythology

Gods and Goddesses

Short Answer

1. Ra.
2. Osiris and Isis.
3. Dionysus.
4. Pan.
5. God and the Devil.
6. The Virgin Mary.
7. In Nepal.
8. Armand said that if God created everything, then he created the Devil, so the vampires, as Children of Satan, were Children of God.
9. The bull.
10. Continuous Awareness.
11. Inanna.
12. It had breasts and a penis.
13. Brother Ninian, who took him to see Columba.
14. Christ's humility and martyrdom for goodness was the ideal of the Taltos.
15. Thor.

Mythology

Multiple Choice

1. C 2. A 3. D 4. D 5. D 6. A 7. B 8. C
9. C 10. D 11. A 12. A 13. C 14. D 15. A

Religious Images

Fill in the Blank

1. Transubstantiation 2. Feast of All Saints 3. Genesis 4. Sister Margaret 5. Lestat 6. Mael 7. Ash Wednesday 8. Franciscans 9. chalice 10. "The word made flesh" 11. Esau 12. Job 13. Joseph 14. Saul 15. Cain

Matching
Match the saints:

1. D 2. G 3. E 4. J 5. H 6. C 7. F 8. B
9. A 10. I

Religion and Mythology Bonus Questions

1. Actaeon's dogs tore him apart and a wild boar killed Adonis.
2. Baal.
3. Ka.
4. Golem.
5. The Feast of St. Michael, or Michelmas.
6. Mircea Eliade.
7. Beltane rituals.
8. Cathars.
9. Diana and Pan.
10. Dis Pater, god of the night.

Chapter Six
The Arts of Darkness

Matching

Paintings

1. A   2. C   3. C   4. E   5. D   6. C   7. B   8. F
9. C   10. C

Film

1. D 2. B 3. H 4. F 5. G 6. F 7. E 8. C
9. A 10. I 11. J 12. K 13. L 14. M 15. P
16. B 17. A 18. N 19. D 20. E 21. B 22. K
23. I 24. O

Poetry

1. D 2. C 3. D 4. G 5. A 6. C 7. E or F
8. D 9. C 10. F

Multiple Choice

1. E 2. E 3. D 4. B 5. B 6. C 7. E 8. C
9. B 10. C 11. A 12. B 13. A 14. A 15. E

Short Answer

1. Charles Dickens.
2. Robert Bloch.
3. Fyodor Dostoevsky.
4. Gulliver.
5. *Macbeth*.
6. Daphne du Maurier.
7. Mephistopheles.
8. Picasso.
9. George Washington Cable.
10. Lestat wore one—his fur-lined cloak.

Matching

1. G 2. B 3. D 4. F 5. C 6. D 7. G 8. C
9. N 10. B 11. K 12. G 13. B 14. H 15. H
16. D 17. A 18. J 19. L or O 20. C 21. I
22. E 23. G 24. M or L 25. E 26. D 27. J
28. G 29. E 30. D

Arts of Darkness Bonus Questions

1. *A Tree Grows in Brooklyn*
2. Elizabeth Barrett Browning
3. The Brontës
4. "Tragic Rabbit"
5. Emmanuel de Witte and Thomas de Keyser
6. *Beauty and the Beast*
7. *Caligula*
8. Keats
9. Punchinello and Harlequin
10. Pierrot

Chapter Seven
What Happened When: History and the Dark Universe

Short Answer

1. Anne Boleyn.
2. The Venerable Bede.
3. The Celts.
4. The stock market crash, followed by the Great Depression.
5. The Picts.
6. Elizabeth I.
7. Alexander the Great.
8. Pope Gregory I.
9. Katherine La Voison and the *Chambre Ardente*.
10. Marie Antoinette.
11. Mozart.
12. The Black Death.
13. The Haitian Revolution.
14. John Knox.
15. Lady Godiva.
16. The Knights Templar.
17. In 563 A. D.
18. Mary Queen of Scots.
19. During the Roman Empire.
20. Vampires must find a way to become anchored in each successive historical period or they will die of boredom or from the inability to change.

Matching

1. H 2. AA 3. N 4. L. 5. Z 6. A 7. E 8. X
9. Y 10. S 11. F 12. O 13. M 14. Q 15. R
16. DD 17. J 18. K 19. D 20. I 21. P 22. T
23. G 24. B 25. W 26. C 27. U 28. V
29. CC 30. BB

Historical Bonus Questions

1. Cornelius Tacitus.
2. Anne Maria van Schurman.
3. *The Book of Kells.*
4. 1943.
5. Julius Caesar.

Chapter Eight
What Happened Where: Geography of the Dark Universe

Short Answer

1. Rice set it on the site of the Elephant Walk Restaurant in the Castro district.
2. Dixie Gates.
3. Alexandria, Egypt.
4. Amsterdam.

5. Kemet means "black soil."
6. From Russia.
7. Villa of the Mysteries in Pompeii.
8. Off the coast of Miami, beyond Fisher Island.
9. Montmartre Cemetery.
10. In the Auvergne.
11. Saqqâra.
12. Grenada.
13. Rome.
14. Georgetown.
15. Boulevard du Temple.
16. Bulgaria.
17. The Gobi.
18. It is where he and Gabreille parted ways and where Marius first came to him.
19. Huayna Pichu.
20. The Cotswolds.
21. Leiden.
22. Martinique.
23. Sonoma.
24. Lynkonos.
25. Divisadero.
26. Naples.
27. Bayou St. Jean.
28. Stonehenge on Salisbury Plain.
29. Gabriel's Oak in St. Martinville, LA.
30. The Cevennes in southern France.

Matching

Match the restaurant:

1. F 2. G 3. A 4. K 5. D 6. E 7. I 8. C
9. H 10. B

Match the hotel:

1. N 2. C 3. G 4. L 5. B 6. M 7. A 8. E
9. J 10. H 11. I 12. O 13. D 14. F 15. K

Match the vampire bar:

1. C 2. A 3. C 4. B 5. D

New Orleans

Multiple Choice

1. A 2. B 3. C 4. C 5. B 6. A 7. C 8. D
9. E 10. C

Paris

True or False

1. F: Lestat stayed in the Ritz, Lasher and Rowan in the George V 2. T 3. T 4. F: He killed the artist in Montmartre 5. F: They chased them into Notre Dame Cathedral 6. T 7. T 8. F: They were at the Palais Royal 9. F: It was on the Boulevard du Temple 10. T

Matching
Match countries and cities:

1. F 2. I 3. G 4. A 5. B 6. P 7. C 8. D
9. H 10. O 11. N 12. J 13. K 14. L 15. M
16. E

Geography Bonus Questions

1. Darkirk.
2. Mekare.
3. The Grand Hotel.
4. An abandoned temple.
5. Fontainebleau.
6. Regent's Park.
7. Napoleonville.

8. The corner suite of the first floor with the fire-place, Number 33.
9. St. Elizabeth's.
10. New Town.

Chapter Nine
Naming Names: Who's Who?

Matching

1. A 2. C 3. H 4. F 5. G 6. I 7. E 8. J
9. D 10. B

Short Answer

1. Davis.
2. Nicolas.
3. CeeCee.
4. Buffoon.
5. By stringing together random syllables, and by observing how he "lashed" the trees.
6. Gentleman Death.
7. *Mojo* is a voodoo charm for protection.
8. Infant Death, Sister Death, or Merciful Death.
9. A lair.
10. Armand.
11. Ratcatcher.
12. Wolfkiller.

13. Ones who return.
14. Jesse.
15. It is required to inherit the legacy.

True or False

1. T   2. F: It was Those Who Want to Die   3. T
4. T   5. F: She pretended to be different women with
the same name   6. T   7. F: It was the name of Michael's previous unborn child   8. T   9. F: It was
Blind Henry   10. F: Carlotta named Deirdre, not
Antha.

Matching

1. H   2. A   3. D   4. F   5. E   6. B   7. I   8. G
9. J   10. C

Who's Who Bonus Questions

1. Jules.
2. Benjamin the Devil.
3. Drinkers of the Blood.
4. Africa.
5. Enchanted Sleep.

Chapter Ten:
Who Said What?

Match the speakers:
(See below for key to title abbreviations.)

1. G (IV 122) 2. J (VL 249) 3. A (IV 142) 4. B
(BT 5) 5. F (IV 69) 6. B (VL 497) 7. L (VL 466)
8. A (IV 168) 9. J (QD 98) 10. I (TS 130) 11. E
(WH 1037) 12. C (TS 386) 13. O (LR 206)
14. D (WH 751) 15. H (WH 932) 16. A (IV 28)
17. P (QD 366) 18. E (WH 13) 19. B (VL 3)
20. T (LR 35) 21. Q (TS 36) 22. H (WH 928)
23. Z (WH 956) 24. D (WH 956) 25. T (LR 12)

Name the character:

1. DD (MM 78) 2. L (VL 362–363) 3. G (IV 104)
4. E (WH 38) 5. N (WH 533) 6. K (WH 4)
7. A (IV 3) 8. M (WH 491) 9. J (IV 239) 10. H
(LR 279) 11. Q (TS 239) 12. X (LR 1) 13. Z
(WH 3) 14. R (LR 139) 15. H (WH 953) 16. A.
(VL 498) 17. S (VL 331) 18. U (VL 129) 19. P

All paperback editions except *Taltos*	BT = *The Tale of the Body Thief*
IV = *Interview with the Vampire* (1977 edition)	WH = *The Witching Hour*
VL = *The Vampire Lestat*	LR = *Lasher*
QD = *The Queen of the Damned*	TS = *Taltos*
	MM = *The Mummy*

(VL 486) 20. O (LR 206) 21. D (WH 171) 22. B
(IV 158) 23. T (LR 14) 24. H (LR 520–521)
25. BB (TS 22) 26. E (WH 68) 27. J (VL 304)
28. B (QD 262) 29. CC (QD 462) 30. P (QD
454)

Bonus Questions

Name the character:

1. Q (TS 200) 2. AA (VL 85) 3. V (LR 107)
4. W (BT 91) 5. C (TS 260)

Match the speakers:

1. U (VL 72) 2. AA (VL 89) 3. Y (TS 454) 4. E
(LR 14) 5. A (IV 13)

Chapter Eleven
Anne Rice

Short Answer

1. October 4, 1941.
2. Mercy Hospital, New Orleans, Louisiana.
3. Howard Allen O'Brien.

4. Alphonsus Liguori—the name of a saint coupled with her aunt's name.

5. She was called Butch as a baby. She changed her name to Anne in the first grade, then to Ellen, then Gracie in the fourth grade. She was also called Barbara Forever in high school, which she is still called sometimes.

6. She moved to Richardson, Texas, when she was sixteen.

7. She was sixteen. He was fifteen.

8. Anne met Stan in journalism class in Richardson, Texas, when he sat down beside her.

9. October 14, 1961.

10. September 21, 1966.

11. March 11, 1978.

12. Political science.

13. Mojo, because she used him in *The Tale of the Body Thief.*

14. Black.

15. Eight and a half, medium, and she has hundreds of pairs of black lace-up shoes.

16. Two. One is a black portable typewriter that she took to college in 1958, and the other is an IBM electric on which she wrote *Interview with the Vampire.*

17. Her stepmother, Dorothy O'Brien.

18. With the best chocolate she can find.

19. Hershey's Milk Chocolate Symphony.

20. In 1979, after *The Feast of All Saints* was published.
21. A rag doll called a Maman doll.
22. She has three sisters and one half-sister.
23. *Last of the Mohicans* with Daniel Day-Lewis.
24. Pumpkinhead.
25. Saint Francis.
26. The one Julia Phillips hosted at Le Dome.
27. Tae kwon do. She takes private lessons from a Korean black belt, and she likes to block and punch.
28. "Because it was there."
29. Ten. One each in Berkeley, Oakland, San Francisco, and Sonoma County, California; one in Seven Points, Texas; one in Destin, Florida; and four in New Orleans—on Philip, First, and Amelia streets, and St. Elizabeth's Orphanage, the largest private residence in the country.
30. In New Orleans, on First Street, the setting for *The Witching Hour*.

The Novels

Short Answer

1. *Belinda*.
2. Michele's.
3. Belinda and Rowan.

4. The scenes of the torture and burning of the women thought to be witches, which Anne researched for Suzanne and Deborah. She had difficulty thinking about and imagining them because they were so brutal.
5. Nathaniel Hawthorne and Henry James.
6. Leonard Wolf.
7. *Dracula's Daughter.*
8. Carlos Castenada.
9. She goes off with some vampire boys who like to bedevil people.
10. About six years.
11. The reversion clause. If the film has not been made after a set amount of time, the rights revert back to Rice.
12. Martians who kill themselves by flying into the sun.
13. Lafayette Cemetery.
14. The Ritz, Paris.
15. From Denton, Texas, to San Francisco.
16. The dog.
17. The actress Charlotte Rampling; Anne loved her looks and poise.
18. *The Claiming of Sleeping Beauty, Beauty's Punishment,* and *Beauty's Release.*
19. *Blade Runner.*
20. *The Empire Strikes Back.*
21. Dr. Robert Owen.
22. He is an artist.

227

23. The line in which Louis says he saw Lestat earlier that year, 1975. Lestat was underground.
24. She thought rock stars were symbolic outsiders, like vampires.
25. *The Vampire Lestat.*
26. John Preston, to whom she dedicated several novels.
27. James M. Cain and Raymond Chandler.
28. The voodoo queen Marie Laveau.
29. "Do you wish to hold the interview here?"
30. Anne got up from her desk with the completed, freshly typed manuscript and was quite excited. She bumped into a tall bookcase. A huge statue of St. Francis of Assisi fell off the bookcase and hit the on/off button of the typewriter, breaking it and totally knocking the typewriter out of service. She wondered if this incident was a warning that the book was evil, but decided it was not because the novel was about peace and love and the ways of gentle as opposed to violent men.

True or False

1. T   2. F: It looks real, but she is too superstitious to have a real skull   3. T   4. T   5. F: It was *Katherine and Jean*   6. F: She wrote it in five weeks   7. F: She wrote about David Bowie   8. T   9. F: She went to St. Joseph's Academy, on which she based her fictional account of St. Rose de Limas   10. T

11. T   12. F: It was *Exit to Eden*   13. T   14. F:
Warner Bros. bought the rights   15. T   16. T   17. T
18. T   19. T   20. F: She published six

Multiple Choice

1. A   2. A   3. D   4. B   5. C   6. A   7. E   8. B
9. A   10. D   11. E   12. C   13. C   14. D   15. B
16. B   17. C   18. E   19. A   20. D

Anne Rice Bonus Questions

1. Twice. During the winter before she moved west
   and during the first winter of her residence in
   1989. Both were unusual for New Orleans, last-
   ing for days, and she used these experiences in
   The Witching Hour.
2. Rice sleeps in a canopied four-poster bed decked
   in gold and purple silk. She wears flannel night-
   gowns made by Lanz of Salzburg. She has
   twenty of them. All are heavy cotton, full length,
   and most have flowers on them.
3. Françoise, the younger sister of Richard Lermontant in *The Feast of All Saints.*
4. She unbuttoned the top button of his shirt because she knew that her father would never have
   been comfortable with the top button buttoned.

She also strongly recommended that he be laid out without a tie, and he was.

5. Brie and macadamia nuts.

Chapter Twelve
The Historical Novels of Anne Rice

The Feast of All Saints

Short Answer

1. Marcel's father was a French-American planter and his mother was half white and half black, so Marcel was considered a quadroon.
2. Christophe Mercier, a writer.
3. Cecile was jealous because Marie could pass for white.
4. Haiti.
5. About 18,000 free people of color lived there in the days before the Civil War.
6. November 1.
7. *Passe blanc* meant that a person of color shared a white ancestry and could pass for white. The *gens* who valued their class and who saw the need for strength in numbers detested those of their race who blended into the white community

and cut off their ties with their family and their people.

8. Cecile burned them.

9. Marcel's family lived in a cottage on St. Anne Street.

10. Marcel resided in the type of building typically reserved for the boys in the family; it is called a *garçonnière*.

11. He drew pictures in which the people looked like ducks.

12. Monsieur de Latte's.

13. Christophe returned from Paris.

14. Melmoth, the wanderer. The vampire Lestat had also used this name as an alias.

15. *Nuits de Charlotte.*

16. Randolph.

17. That someone was offering money for the stage rights and wanted Christophe to adapt it.

18. St. Charles Hotel—the same place that Stuart Townsend and Arthur Langtry stayed in *The Witching Hour.*

19. Twenty.

20. Seven feet tall.

21. Lockjaw.

22. One dollar.

23. Jules Lion.

24. He was Marcel's white father.

25. Monsieur Jacquemine.

26. The parish of St. Jacques.

27. The history of ancient Rome.
28. Ophelia.
29. An antique *secrétaire* that belonged to his wife. Marie gave it to Anna Bella, who showed it to Vincent Dazincourt, Philippe's wife's brother. Vincent then told his sister that Philippe had stolen it from her.
30. *Plaçage* was the alliance of a white man with a woman of color. The man agreed to set her and her children up with a house and an income in return for her sexual favors.

Fill in the Blank

1. *Robinson Crusoe* 2. Rome 3. *L'Album Litteraire*, a book of poems written by free men of color 4. without care 5. St. Augustine 6. five 7. Marguerite 8. the "tignon law" 9. August 15 10. Hamilton

True or False

1. T 2. F: Vincent fought several duels on Marie's behalf, but he only warned Christophe that he nearly had to fight a duel with Captain Hamilton since Christophe could not do it himself 3. T 4. F: It was Richard's grandfather who devised the plan 5. T 6. T 7. F: Lisette took Marie to Madame Lola, a voodooienne, who sold her to several white men for

the night   8. T   9. F: His father wanted him to do this, but he refused   10. T

Cry to Heaven

Fill in the Blank

1. six   2. Caracena, Italy   3. eighteen (in 1727)
4. Caracena   5. judge; he was a member of the Council of Three   6. Marc Antonio Treschi   7. Lena
8. father (although he pretended to be his brother)
9. painting   10. Andrea Treschi   11. "Long live the knife" (an affirmation of the greatness of castrated singers)   12. bauta   13. Cafferelli   14. Brenta
15. Andrea's valet

Short Answer

1. Alessandro.
2. The first girl with whom Tonio had sex; she was a tavern girl.
3. His lost voice.
4. He hanged himself in his prison cell.
5. The Neapolitan Conservatorio San Angelo.
6. In Florence.
7. An incubus.
8. Mount Vesuvius.
9. Two weeks.

10. Cellino.
11. The ability to forgive.
12. A trunk that contained items from his childhood, such as his christening gowns.
13. She was the dressmaker for his stage performances.
14. Lagrimi Christi.
15. Five hundred ducats.
16. The Teatro Argentina.
17. Guido's first full-production opera, staged in Rome.
18. Ganymede.
19. In a fencing salon.
20. The count provided "bravos," or armed bodyguards.
21. The girl.
22. They were cousins.
23. She was an artist.
24. During Lent.
25. (e) large eyes (Tonio just happens to have large eyes).

Historical Fiction Bonus Questions

1. The Feast of All Saints is a day of remembering the dead so they are not lost; the novel is a way to keep the free people of color from becoming lost in obscurity.

2. Four years old.
3. "God triumphs in the ruins of our plan."
4. The *New Orleans Daily Picayune.*
5. Girod Cemetery.
6. Alessandro Moreschi.
7. Tonio's duet with the Contessa in Naples.
8. The Golden Book.
9. The Oracle of Delphi.
10. Eden.

Chapter Thirteen
The Erotica of Anne Rampling

Exit to Eden

Fill in the Blank

1. The Perfectionist 2. five foot nine inches
3. Berkeley 4. Diana 5. *The Club Gazette* 6. Eden
7. Mr. Cross 8. *Elysium* 9. *Angelo, My Love*
10. Parliament 100s

Short Answer

1. Lisa favored Bombay Gin.
2. Fifteen.

3. A doctorate in English literature from the University of California at Berkeley.

4. Elliott published two books of photojournalism, *San Francisco Tenderloin: Down and Out* and *Beirut: Twenty-Four Hours*. He gave Lisa the latter after she took it from his suitcase and removed the plastic wrap.

5. When he signed the book, he told her he loved her.

6. Twenty-four.

7. A membership fee of $250,000.

8. Lisa wanted to name her new invention the Eden Express, after the Orient Express. She imagined it decked out in Edwardian furnishings, and pulled by a steam engine.

9. Three thousand, approximately three-quarters full.

10. A waterbug.

11. Chanel.

12. Texas.

13. At Billy Bob's Texas.

14. Bonnie and Clyde.

15. Scott and Richard.

16. Lisa told Martin Halifax that he could find her at the Marie Laveau Court on the Rue St. Anne, registered under the name "Mrs. Elliott Slater."

17. Eudora Welty wrote the story, "The Death of a Traveling Salesman."

18. The Royal Danieli Excelsior.

19. In Berkeley, California, when she came to his house to tell him she loved him.
20. In Cannes; in a church.

Multiple Choice

1. D   2. D   3. A   4. C   5. B   6. D   7. A   8. B
9. B   10. D

Belinda

Short Answer

1. A Catholic schoolgirl's outfit, with pleated skirt and knee socks.
2. Not to ask about her past or her parents.
3. She was a professional novelist.
4. *Crimson Mardi Gras.*
5. Jody.
6. Black Russians.
7. A pallet.
8. Twice.
9. In Haight Ashbury, on Page Street.
10. An MG-TD roadster.
11. Becky Thatcher.
12. Linda Merit.
13. Representational.
14. Andy Blatky.

15. *Dolly Rose.*
16. Eighteen.
17. A major art collector who buys four of Jeremy's paintings of Belinda.
18. The leopard skin coat.
19. Midnight Mink.
20. Horn-rimmed glasses.
21. Roaches and rats.
22. "Champagne Flight."
23. Marty Moreshi.
24. Fire Island.
25. To St. Margaret's in Gstaad, Switzerland.
26. St. Charles Avenue.
27. An old mansion that Rice remembered from childhood, now torn down.
28. Twenty-eight.
29. *Belinda on the Carousel Horse.*
30. Bru.

Fill in the Blank

1. Bonnie Sinclair   2. Alex Flint   3. Algonquin
4. November 7   5. Florence, Italy   6. Goldilocks
7. Prince Charming   8. Rumpelstiltskin   9. Texas
10. Seventeenth   11. Rodeo Drive   12. St. Francis
13. *Looking for Bettina*   14. seven   15. fifteen
16. Miss Annie   17. Carmel   18. twenty-two
19. *Final Score*   20. Rembrandt

Anne Rampling Bonus Questions

1. Balkan Sobranie.
2. Elliott did not have the third book in the Roque-laure trilogy, *Beauty's Release*, because it was not yet published. *Exit to Eden* came out in 1985, just ahead of *Beauty's Release*.
3. The Roissy Academy, which is a code name for the house mentioned in *The Story of O*.
4. Sir Richard Burton.
5. Road Warrior.
6. Jeremy's father, Dr. Walker, volunteered to go to war and was killed in the South Pacific two months after Jeremy was born.
7. He kept the keys in a white opaque spice jar in the kitchen marked "Rosemary."
8. Roasted chicken.
9. Stanford Court.
10. Philosophy.

Super Bonus Questions

Matching
Match the physicians:

1. C 2. D 3. F 4. A 5. G 6. E 7. B 8. H
or B

Match the First Street help:

1. O 2. B 3. C 4. G 5. E 6. H 7. A 8. D
9. J 10. I 11. F 12. N 13. L 14. M 15. K
16. P

Short Answer

1. Berenice.
2. One of Mary Beth's "boys."
3. Eileen.
4. Michael Curry's high school girlfriend.
5. He was Ryan Mayfair's house servant in Metairie.
6. The Huguenots.
7. Marie and Virginie.
8. He was Marguerite's mulatto coachman and thought to be the bastard son of Marguerite's son, Louis-Pierre. He is a Mayfair by five lines of descent.
9. Arthur Langtry.

10. She was the woman who died in the hospital bed that Michael Curry occupied after his near-death experience. He knows her name via psychometry.

11. Sluggo.

12. *War and Peace*.

13. Gun Barrel City, Texas.

14. Carlos.

15. Celeste.

16. A miniature coffin.

17. His construction company.

18. Violet.

19. Denis.

20. The *Marianna*.

21. Lestat threw it into the ocean, but David rescued it and brought it to the town house.

22. Monet.

23. Uruk.

24. Harry.

25. He was Antoine Fontenay's manservant.

26. Jimmy Barnes.

27. Comtessa de Chamillart.

28. Salamander.

29. Indigo.

30. Duchess Anna, a whore.

31. A friend of Charlotte's at court, who insisted to Petyr van Abel that she could not be a witch.

32. A .38-caliber Smith and Wesson revolver with a long barrel.

33. Oliver Stone's *JFK*.
34. Three hundred.
35. "To learn to tap dance and to be able to do it in a white furry cat costume." She is looking for a private tutor and has already designed the costume.

True or False

1. T   2. F: Anton Marcus replaced David Talbot
3. F: He thinks the style is like Caravaggio   4. F: He was called the Back Street Strangler   5. T   6. F: *The Wind Singer* was his first boat   7. T   8. F: The constellation is the Pleiades, or the Seven Sisters   9. T
10. F: It sold over four million copies   11. F: Marius called Lestat Brat Prince   12. T   13. F: Her room number was 203   14. T   15. F: She was born at Mercy Hospital

Bibliography

Ramsland, Katherine. *Prism of the Night: A Biography of Anne Rice.* New York: Dutton, 1991.

————. *The Vampire Companion: The Official Guide to Anne Rice's "The Vampire Chronicles."* New York: Ballantine, 1993.

————. *The Witches' Companion: The Official Guide to Anne Rice's "Lives of the Mayfair Witches."* New York: Ballantine, 1994.

Rice, Anne. *Interview with the Vampire.* New York: Ballantine, 1977.

————. *The Feast of All Saints.* New York: Ballantine, 1991.

————. *Cry to Heaven.* New York: Ballantine, 1991.

————. *The Vampire Lestat.* New York: Ballantine, 1986.

————. *The Queen of the Damned.* New York: Ballantine, 1989.

———. *The Mummy*. New York: Ballantine, 1989.

———. *The Witching Hour*. New York: Ballantine, 1991.

———. *The Tale of the Body Thief*. New York: Ballantine, 1993.

———. *Lasher*. New York: Ballantine, 1994.

———. *Taltos*. New York: Knopf, 1994.

Rice, Anne (as Anne Rampling). *Exit to Eden*. New York: Morrow, 1985.

———. *Belinda*. New York: Morrow, 1986.